Things Get Rearranged

Things Get Rearranged

HOW E. DUDLEY PARSONS AND HIS
PASSION FOR JUSTICE SENT ME
FROM MINNESOTA TO MOSCOW

Janet Parsons Mackey

For My Family

From Generation to Generation

Acknowledgements

———

I COULDN'T HAVE WRITTEN ANY of these essays without my teachers. Thanks go to Sara Brenner for guiding me toward some key understandings, which continue to inform me. Kathleen Olesky, Kathy Nutt, and Cheryl Sommers Aubin were first writing teachers who encouraged me at the beginning. Above all, I'm grateful to Joanne Lozar Glenn, a gifted writer, skillful teacher, and empathic critic. Her constant support and challenges continue to teach me. I wouldn't have persisted without her.

Thank you to my brothers Dudley and Rolf Parsons, who read and responded to these memoir-essays about our grandfather, E. Dudley Parsons, Sr. Both offered observations and corrections. Although my sister Carol and brother James are no longer alive, they, too, contributed to my quest for understanding. I'm immensely grateful to my son Eric, who provided endless help with the family tree, neighborhood map, and family photographs.

Members of writing groups and friends provided supportive criticism: Barbara, DiAna, Duffie, Evelyn, Mary, Marge, Ramona, Ruth, Stephanie, and Urmilla. Thank you, writers, for your thoughtful reading and feedback. Hearty appreciation goes to Jan and Tom, who read through an early draft, and offered useful comments and ideas. Still other readers came to my aid: Katie, Susanne, Doug, Betty, Gayle and Marci. Marci's attention to detail pointed to spots where clarification was needed. I've incorporated some suggestions from all these allies, pondered others, and take full responsibility for the final outcome.

Various public servants provided gracious help. Ms. Marci Matson, Director of Edina Historical Society, gave me access to family items in their collection, in addition to her critical review of my draft. Ms. Mary Raabe, steady volunteer at Hopkins Historical Society, was generous backup for my search through issues of *The Hennepin County Review*. I also thank a multitude of librarians for their good cheer and encouragement, which they gave as staff members in the following libraries: Fairfax County (Virginia) Public Library, Library of Congress, Fresno California Public Library, The Hennepin County Library and Minneapolis Public Library, Minnesota Historical Society, Minnesota Legislative Reference Library, and St. Paul Minnesota Public Library. They all responded promptly to my inquiries, and pointed me in fruitful directions.

Thank you.

"Tell the . . . truth, but tell it slant...."

Emily Dickinson

Table of Contents

To the Reader

———

I BEGAN THESE PERSONAL ESSAYS for my grandchildren, their children, other family members, and friends. Later, I thought they might appeal to anyone interested in a liberal corner of Minnesota during an earlier time in our history. Other readers, curious about the transmission of culture through several generations, might also enjoy these stories. Whether they are read or not, I have benefited. I understand more about my grandparents and their times. I've learned about myself, and my own choices. I've gained perspective through mining my imperfect but honest memory. I've become enriched through attempting to describe my experience of my grandparents.

While working on this collection, I tried to keep focus on my grandfather, whose personality and convictions had an impact on our family. It would have been futile to attempt to disguise places or family names, although I made an exception for some minor characters to protect their privacy. I also need to clear up confusion about family names. My grandfather's name was Ernest Dudley Parsons, known as E. Dudley Parsons. My father's given name was Dudley Parsons; later, he added the "E" – but not the full "Ernest," and became known as E. Dudley Parsons, Jr. My brother's birth certificate names him as Ernest Dudley Parsons III, although this is technically incorrect. This information matters in the citations, primarily, for in the stories they are Grandpa, Dad, and Dudley.

As my pile of stories grew, I began to see them as a collage. The resulting picture of my grandfather is more like a cubist painting, in which certain planes are prominent or exaggerated. It's less like a classic portrait, in which details are finely rendered, and all viewers recognize the person.

At the front of this book, I include a quote from Emily Dickinson: "Tell...the truth, but tell it slant...." In fact, she wrote, "Tell *all* the truth..." [Italics added.] These essays couldn't include *all* the truth. The biographical notes in the appendix, which my father had compiled, reveal how much is left out. They point to experiences and information missing from family stories. Moreover, my essays comprise only a portion of my own family experience. My grandmother, who was gifted and energetic, doesn't appear in proportion to her influence. I have yet to tell her story, or trace its possible line in my children and their families. I've pondered, too, how my son Eric fits into this collection. It seems to me that he exemplifies other portions of the family inheritance, perhaps my grandmother's legacy. In any case, much remains for further exploration.

I ask: how much *can* one discern about another family member? I might have understood more, had I conversed with others who'd known my grandparents. I regret the lost opportunity. Besides, people reveal only portions of their inner beings, to others as well as to themselves, in differing and conflicting measure. And those who view others will do so through their own filters. In the end, it's not possible to pin down, label, or box in others, and especially not my grandfather. His motives and choices will always retain an element of mystery. That mystery is to be honored.

I do know this: I first felt his personality, his enthusiasms, and his politics during the years my father, my siblings, and I lived in our grandparents' home in the Village of Morningside, Minnesota, just outside the Minneapolis city limits.

On account of Grandpa, I learned that stories could speed through generations to influence me as a Parsons. His tales spurred curiosity, provided context, taught behavior, exuded liveliness, and burnished an expectation of adventure. His reminiscences carried values: ideas matter, an open book invites one into a new world, conversation can birth new perspectives.

Because of Grandpa, I became aware of equal rights for people of color. I heard about political efforts for fair wages, free speech, and open debate. I awoke to these issues during a transition time. It was a transition in my own life, from childhood innocence to a period of painful growth. At the same time, America was changing from a period of World War II alliances to Cold War hostility.

Although these essays spring from *my* memory, *my* experience, I've also mined Grandpa's own writing: newspaper columns, books, letters to editors, and more than six years' correspondence with my parents while we lived in India. I've deepened my perceptions of his personality because of this rich material. I've rounded my views of the social contexts in which my family lived. These archives helped me to "Try to enter the past without blaming it for lacking the present perspective," as pastor and historian Mary Luti once suggested during a retreat I attended in Chartres, France. Others, who might have known Grandpa or read his material, will differ in some perceptions.

During the McCarthy Era, our family moved into a darker place than that which I first knew with my grandparents. We used the tool of silence to bury painful memories. We also covered up the bright times he brought and exemplified. When I began these pieces, I was attempting to understand more about him, and his impact upon my family. Now, I also want to invite him back into the family circle that we might appreciate and honor him at last.

I hope family history won't stay buried forever. Someone will become curious, as I have been; others might follow in Grandpa's footsteps without recognizing they've done so. I'm fascinated with ways in which his ideals have surfaced in different family members. I've wondered about the connections between Grandpa's fierce commitment to Progressive politics, economic justice, and his early enthusiasm for the Russian Revolution with my younger son's interest in Russia, where he's studied and worked. It's curious that my family expanded to include my daughter-in-law Olga, who grew up in the USSR, and my grandchildren Dylan and Jessica, who live and speak in a bilingual household. And now it's become my turn. I've joined other family members in learning about Russia's complex history and culture. I marvel that my family's legacy has led to such positive outcomes.

I want my grandchildren to meet their great-great-grandfather.

Janet Parsons Mackey, 2015

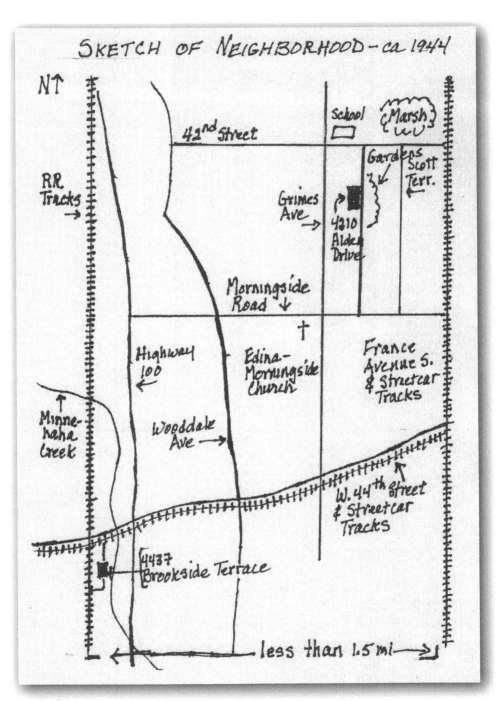

Sketch of Neighborhood – ca. 1944

Family Tree – Parsons Line

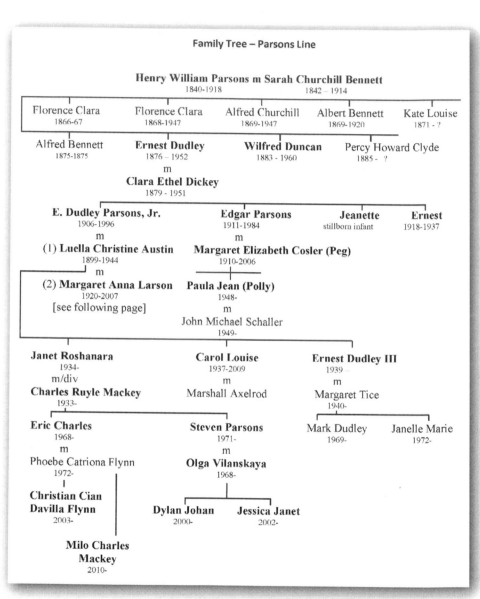

Henry William Parsons m Sarah Churchill Bennett
1840-1918   1842 – 1914

Florence Clara	Florence Clara	Alfred Churchill	Albert Bennett	Kate Louise
1866-67	1868-1947	1869-1947	1869-1920	1871 - ?

Alfred Bennett	**Ernest Dudley**	**Wilfred Duncan**	Percy Howard Clyde
1875-1875	1876 – 1952	1883 - 1960	1885 - ?

m

Clara Ethel Dickey
1879 - 1951

E. Dudley Parsons, Jr.	**Edgar Parsons**	**Jeanette**	**Ernest**
1906-1996	1911-1984	stillborn infant	1918-1937

m   m

(1) Luella Christine Austin   **Margaret Elizabeth Cosler (Peg)**
1899-1944   1910-2006

m

(2) Margaret Anna Larson   Paula Jean (Polly)
1920-2007   1948-
[see following page]   m

John Michael Schaller
1949-

Janet Roshanara	**Carol Louise**	**Ernest Dudley III**
1934-	1937-2009	1939 –
m/div	m	m
Charles Ruyle Mackey	Marshall Axelrod	Margaret Tice
1933-		1940-

Eric Charles	**Steven Parsons**	Mark Dudley	Janelle Marie
1968-	1971-	1969-	1972-
m	m		
Phoebe Catriona Flynn	**Olga Vilanskaya**		
1972-	1968-		

Christian Cian Davilla Flynn
2003-

Dylan Johan	**Jessica Janet**
2000-	2002-

Milo Charles Mackey
2010-

Family Tree – Parsons Line

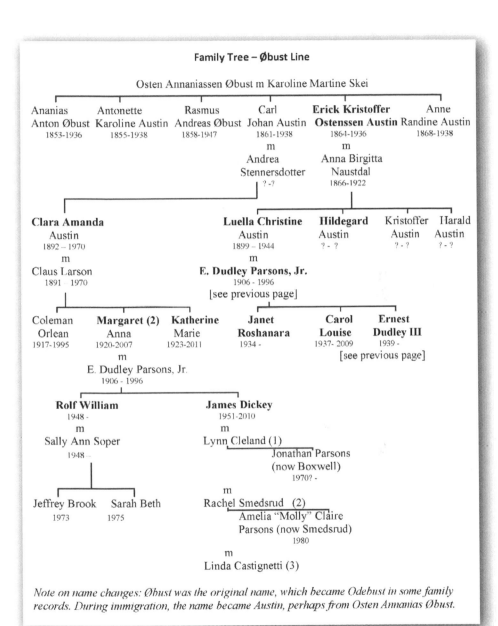

Family Tree – Øbust Line

Osten Annaniassen Øbust m Karoline Martine Skei

| Ananias Anton Øbust 1853-1936 | Antonette Karoline Austin 1855-1938 | Rasmus Andreas Øbust 1858-1947 | Carl Johan Austin 1861-1938 m Andrea Stennersdotter ? -? | Erick Kristoffer Ostenssen Austin 1864-1936 m Anna Birgitta Naustdal 1866-1922 | Anne Randine Austin 1868-1938 |

| **Clara Amanda** Austin 1892 – 1970 m Claus Larson 1891   1970 | **Luella Christine** Austin 1899 – 1944 m **E. Dudley Parsons, Jr.** 1906 - 1996 [see previous page] | **Hildegard** Austin ? - ? | Kristoffer Austin ? - ? | Harald Austin ? - ? |

| Coleman Orlean 1917-1995 | **Margaret (2)** Anna 1920-2007 m E. Dudley Parsons, Jr. 1906 - 1996 | **Katherine** Marie 1923-2011 | **Janet Roshanara** 1934 - | **Carol Louise** 1937- 2009 | **Ernest Dudley III** 1939 - [see previous page] |

| **Rolf William** 1948 - m Sally Ann Soper 1948 — | **James Dickey** 1951-2010 m Lynn Cleland (1) |

Jonathan Parsons (now Boxwell) 1970? -

| Jeffrey Brook 1973 | Sarah Beth 1975 |

m
Rachel Smedsrud   (2)

Amelia "Molly" Claire Parsons (now Smedsrud) 1980

m
Linda Castignetti (3)

Note on name changes: Øbust was the original name, which became Odebust in some family records. During immigration, the name became Austin, perhaps from Osten Annanias Øbust.

Family Tree – Øbust Line

CHAPTER 1
Mystery Clues

———

WHY DOESN'T MY FAMILY TALK about our grandfather? His presence feels strong – I hear him now, delivering opinions about the news. I know he's influenced other family members, yet we rarely refer to him. Do we muffle his voice with our noisy attention to meals, homework, childcare, meeting agendas, office balance sheets, or house repairs? Is it that, as the eldest of his six grandchildren and now a grandmother myself, I'm the only one who cares about holding the vivid memories? Or, *is* he discussed, while I'm out of the loop far from Minnesota? I'd asked these questions for many years. But by the summer of 2010, my parents and stepmother Margaret were all dead, as were my sister Carol and brother James. Dudley, Rolf, and I are aging. It had become time to learn more.

"What do you remember about Grandpa?" I was on one of my regular visits to Minnesota, spending time with my brother Dudley and his family, in their Rochester home. He was younger than I by four years, and the sibling most likely to recall when I was nine, and he five, at the time we moved into our grandparents' home on Alden Drive in Morningside.

"I remember being shaken like a rag doll when he saw me chewing gum." His voice became louder. I caught my breath, jolted in my gut, wondering how this piece could fit into my grandfather-puzzle.

1

"He thought I'd been chewing gum during Sunday School," Dudley explained, "but I wasn't. It was after I got home from church."

Where were we? I was probably sitting on the couch, next to Dudley's recliner in his family room. My brother's memory recalled my grandfather's impetuous side. Grandpa's shaking Dudley reminded me that Grandpa's passions often combined with principle – in this case keeping the Sabbath Day holy. It's as if that commandment overtook Grandpa's kindness – why else would one shake a child "like a rag doll?"

"Keep the Sabbath Day holy." That was a given in my grand-parents' household. That's why Sunday dinners were so important, and Sunday visitors, and gentle activities such as naps, afternoon tea, and summertime walks. The Fourth Commandment also meant that Dad wasn't allowed to read the Sunday comics when he was young. "I had a paper route, so when I was getting the papers ready to deliver, I went behind the wood shed and read the comics there." Dad told this story several times, always pleased at his deception. The stricture must have boosted his resolve. And there was fall-out: as long as I lived at home, it was impossible to read Sunday comics first. No matter how early I got up, Dad was looking at them while sipping his breakfast coffee. Today, in my own home, I begin with comics on Sunday mornings.

"And I remember the pigeon." My brother brought me back to the couch.

"Omigod, I'd forgotten about the pigeon."

We rehearsed the story and wove it together. Grandpa had walked in the front door close to suppertime, swinging a dead pi-geon by its legs. He was on his way home from work when he saw a car strike the bird, whipping it, so it landed close to the curb. He grabbed the dead creature, climbed onto a streetcar, arrived home and presented it to Grandma. He was excited, as if some primal hunter had been awakened. "It was *freshly* killed!" That's how I imagine his justifying his gift. He expected her to cook it for dinner. Grandma refused. She would have responded "*No*, E.D." (That's what she called him when she needed to be firm; in worse cases it was "Mr. Parsons.")

Then Dudley capped the story: "He cooked it! He fried it! It was awful."

That wasn't the only trophy Grandpa brought home. The garden urn was the most treasured by our family. As we sat there, I could see it outside Dudley's sliding door. We'll never figure out how Grandpa managed to get it home without a heart attack. I don't know when this triumph occurred, because the urn was "always there." Grandpa had been selling life insurance door to door in a Minneapolis neighborhood of fine old homes. As he neared one of these houses, a workman came out of the yard with a black cast iron urn in a wheelbarrow. When Grandpa learned that it was on its way to a dump, he commandeered it and hailed a taxi. He and the driver wrestled it into the trunk and delivered it to 4210 Alden Drive. My grandfather had to have been overtaken with desire for the urn, and shocked that it wouldn't be preserved. He wouldn't have paid cab fare for a frivolous purpose.

This beauty, about three feet across and just as high, is a reproduction of an urn at Versailles, my family has always said. We've verified this piece of the lore, during two separate trips to France, when family members located the original on the terrace of Versailles Palace. The King's vessel matches our possession. It features two satyrs sitting on opposite sides. Their human hands grasp the rim, their goat legs clasp the bowl, their curly heads with blank eyes regard each other across prolific flowers. My grandmother changed plantings each year, having started them from seed, or from trading plants with neighbors. I remember its sitting on a level place in their front yard, not far from the sloping pathway to the back.

3

When the house was sold in 1951, Dad and our stepmother Margaret moved the urn to 4437 Brookside Terrace. There it stayed near the rose garden for fifty more years, filled with blossoms each summer. There were petunias, grasses, and trailing ivy, but since Margaret loved gardening, she probably varied the plantings. Now it graces my brother's back yard in a shady spot, visible from their family room. It must weigh 200 pounds; it took three men to load and unload it from Dudley's van. And my grandfather had done this with a captive taxi driver!

Several days after visiting Dudley, I asked my question of my still younger brother Rolf. "What do you remember about Grandpa?" Rolf was born in 1948, after we moved to Brookside Terrace, so he would have been four when Grandpa died. He shared three dim recollections. "I remember we made a scrap-book about horses." Grandpa had a gentle side, and would want to see a child improve his mind. He and Rolf were in Grandpa's room while Margaret tended to housework. I wonder where they found pictures of horses for Rolf to cut out with his blunt-nosed scissors. *Crik, crik, crik* as Grandpa bent his head to watch with his one eye.

"I remember he lay in his new room when he was sick," Rolf added. This room had been added to the house, just for Grandpa. It overlooked the lawn sloping down to the banks of Minnehaha Creek. His tenure in that room was too brief – ten months between his return from Europe and his death from pancreatic cancer.

"And I remember a sound coming from that room during suppertime, and everyone got up to go to him." He must have needed pain medication or a sip of water. Perhaps he was having a morphine nightmare.

That's all I could unearth. Later, I asked each brother if they recalled any discussion about Grandpa's political opinions. Dudley responded "I was too young to have been involved early, before his death, so I don't recall it as a forbidden topic." Rolf wrote, "His politics were never discussed."

One of my questions is answered: "*Is* he discussed, while I am out of the loop, far from Minnesota?" There is no loop.

But there is a legacy.

304 East 48th Street, Minneapolis, Minnesota

CHAPTER 2

June 6, 1944

———

IT WAS A LATE WINTER day in 1944, soon after my ninth birthday. Dad was home, maybe right after teaching school, maybe on a Sunday afternoon. It was dark.

It was dark and cold in Minnesota, but he asked me if I wanted a hot fudge sundae. *Yes, I did.* It wasn't far to the ice cream parlor – we walked there in the summer eager for a five-cents, one-scoop cone. Even in cold weather, it wasn't far. Anyway, we didn't have a car.

My glasses steamed up as we entered the warm store and sat down in a brown leather booth across the aisle from fogged windows. A few other customers were eating and talking. Dad ordered coffee for himself, and a hot fudge sundae for me – a luxury for a family careful with money.

I dipped my spoon into the tall glass. Fudge ran over the rim, and I stopped it with my fingers, licking off the goo. Dad cleared his throat, began to speak, hesitated, and started over. Then: "I have something to tell you. Your mother's not going to get well." *Yes, she would. In heaven.* That internal response was swift. My Sunday School teachers had said that when good people die they go to a place called "heaven," where everything is all right. In my gut, where the ice cream wouldn't melt, I knew my mother had been getting worse. Perhaps I was holding onto a hope that couldn't be fulfilled at home, so placed it far into the future, far above earth.

But to Dad, I made no reply. I nodded in silence, and took a few more spoonsful. Then I wasn't hungry anymore.

Dad finished his coffee. We left to walk home along the unlit wartime streets, without talking. Dad's statement hadn't been a surprise. I'd seen my mother carry on after her mastectomy four years before. At first, everything seemed normal again with its predictable routine of meals, school, and playtime. At bedtime she came into our room to say good night. My sister Carol and I shared a double bed; my brother Dudley's crib was against the wall. In the dark, Mother and I said together the Bible verse from Isaiah she helped me memorize. "But they that wait upon the Lord shall renew their strength; they shall mount up with wings as eagles; they shall run and not be weary; and they shall walk, and not faint." [1]

During the previous fall, she had to master cooking and cleaning from a wheelchair, turning her wheels to move from table to stove, as she scraped carrots and put them into stew. Physicians told her she had arthritis in her spine. Next came Christmastime, when she lay on the daybed in the dining room and asked for a mirror, to see the reflected decorated tree behind her. That was the year when "church ladies," from St. John's Lutheran Church, gave us presents – mine was a set of hand-sewn clothes for Marcia, my doll. I sat on the floor near the Christmas tree's low branches and dressed her immediately. I glanced at Dad and saw his grim look. Why did he look that way, when Marcia had such nice clothing? Was it wrong to have gifts from someone we didn't know? I thought, when much older, that he'd looked unhappy because we'd received charity,

After Christmas, my mother lay in the bedroom with curtains pulled against the light, waiting for morphine, getting morphine, sleeping, waking, and being alert for a while. We could talk with her, then. Once I gave her a sponge bath, washing her scarred chest as she leaned against the pillows in late afternoon light.

And one night I crawled into bed with her, next to her warm paralyzed body, to receive surprising news about menstruation: "Don't be afraid when the blood comes. It's normal. You can ask someone for help." I felt happy to be close, hearing these secrets of growing up. Did I realize – somehow – that she was preparing me to be without her? These moments of being together were brief; she'd need the morphine again. Her alert times were insertions into our days filled with eating, school, playmates, sleeping, and a free-floating confusion. It was normal: a routine structured our days. But it wasn't normal: our mother lay in a bedroom, not present to us.

Different relatives came to help, taking turns for weeks at a time. These were our cousins Margaret, her sister, and Aunt Hildegard. Carol and I continued with school, church and playmates, while our young brother Dudley stayed home. "Housekeepers" filled in, between their war-factory jobs. The fat one with yellow hair and two spots of misapplied rouge fed us canned tomato soup and peanut butter sandwiches for lunch. Every day – that's what it felt like.

One day the household was agitated when we arrived home from school. A neighbor from across the alley – my friend's mom, a nurse – was in the kitchen, offering help. Several other adults moved in and out of the dark room where my mother lay. Dad was on the phone. And then Grandma arrived, after walking from Alden Drive in suburban Morningside to France Avenue. There she took the streetcar to Lake Street, transferred to the Lake Street line, and then again onto the Nicollet Avenue line. At East 48th Street she finally began the walk to our house. She meant to retrieve us three children, reverse the journey with us, and comfort us in her Morningside home. No one gave us the reason for these plans, even though my seven-year-old sister and I were never taken out of school midweek. Perhaps they assumed we knew what was going on.

But I refused. "No, I want to go to school tomorrow."
Both Dad and Grandma tried to change my mind.
"I want to go to school."
Grandma offered ideas about how she'd take care of us. I stood there and waited them out. "I have to go to school." That was my safe place. My friend's mother emerged from the kitchen to suggest that I stay overnight in their home across the back alley, and her offer relieved us all. They decided that Grandma should take Carol and five-year-old Dudley on the three-streetcar-trip. I would walk a few yards to my friend's back door.

In the morning, my friend and I ate breakfast at a square table in their kitchen, covered by sunlight. She started to giggle when she spilled sugar onto her scrambled eggs: "Well, I didn't *mean* to do it." Her mother was frowning but calm, as my friend's hand brushed the sugar grains onto the tabletop. Even now I can see individual grains slide off her plate, as if in slow motion. We finished eating and left for school.

When we walked into the front hallway of Eugene Field Elementary School, my fourth-grade teacher was waiting on the polished wooden floors. She took my face into her two hands, looked at me with her brown eyes, and surrounded me with her distinctive scent.

"Oh, my dear." And then, seeing my confusion, "Oh! She doesn't know."

She led me into the classroom to start the day. Probably I found my seat at the wooden desk with its iron legs, inkwell, and lift-top. Likely I saw the cursive alphabet crawling along the upper blackboard edge. After that, attendance, the Pledge of Allegiance, the collection of tin foil for the war, the news of the day (the Allies were invading Normandy), the reading lesson. With this pattern, the day was becoming steady and predictable. But the Principal came into the classroom. My father had called. I was to be sent home.

I walked home by myself and arrived at the front door. My sister and brother were there – Grandma must have returned with them. Carol and Dudley sat together on the porch swing, feet dangling. My father asked me to sit with them. He knelt on the gray floorboards, one knee down, the other one up. His long tapered fingers rested on his thigh. He cleared his throat. "I have bad news. Your mother has died." I stared at him, stone-faced, then checked my sister and brother. Carol's eyes were brimming over. Dudley looked bewildered. Over sixty-five years later, I don't know what I was feeling, if indeed I permitted myself any feelings at the time. Just: *it's over.* Decades later, I astonished myself when describing my mother's death by bursting into tears and weeping like a toddler. Or a nine-year-old.

After that, Grandma must have whisked us away to her home, my safe place for the next three years. Next there was a funeral at St. John's Lutheran Church. My still, cold mother lay in an open casket under the stained glass window of Jesus the Good Shepherd, who was carrying a lamb. I heard the pastor describe her as a good woman. When I saw her lying there, it was a comfort – a chance to see her again. After the funeral, we must have been driven to a church cemetery in rural Minnesota. She is buried there near her own mother, who also died of breast cancer. My mother had lived for forty-four years.

When I step back and look at that time, I ask: *who would let a child walk home from school alone when that child's mother has just died?* Maybe I wasn't alone, but that's my memory. During World War II, we took that walk four times a day without escort, and I suppose the school couldn't spare anyone. I ask: *who could talk with children about her impending death?* In one of my mother's letters to a friend, she indicated my parents struggle: " . . .they are all young and very little has been said. I don't want them all stirred and yet there are so many things I want to say."[2] After I became a mother myself, I recalled bits of kindness and support extended to me. A teacher had taken me Christmas shopping to help me choose a handkerchief for my mother. Grandma and Grandpa came to visit, bringing enthusiasm about us, their grandchildren. Eventually I knew that all the adults surrounding us did the best they could to help us through those difficult, difficult months.

For years I carried a feeling I couldn't name: I wouldn't be alive after my own forty-fourth year. I lived with an "on-hold" undertone, even though I was active and engaged. I still don't eat canned tomato soup, and rarely close curtains in my home – I need to let in the light. And when I turned forty-four I was astonished: I could see a future and claim it! I chose a vocation as a pastor, and later specialized in helping churches deal with loss. I tasted peanut butter again. And now I love to share hot fudge sundaes with my grandchildren.

4210 Alden Drive, Morningside, Minnesota

CHAPTER 3
Dinnertime

———

SOME OF MY MEMORIES ARE SO vivid they are present as images. They're visual recalls; those of our dinnertimes are especially strong.

It's two o'clock on Sunday and we've seated ourselves at table. Grandpa's back is to the bay window framing both him and the back yard garden. The tall corner cupboard on his left holds the Havilland dinnerware brought out for high occasions: Thanksgiving, Christmas, Easter, bridge club, and family reunions. Sunday dinner isn't a high occasion, but we do set the table properly: silverware one inch from the table's edge, glass for water or milk at knife's tip, and napkin folded at the left. Grandma's reason was, "You can just pick it up by the corner and in one motion unfold it onto your lap." She sits at the other end of the table, opposite Grandpa. To her left is the arched niche housing precious objects on the several shelves. On one of these is the tea caddy holding Great-Grandfather Edgar Van Buren Dickey's Civil War medals.

This is our gathering place for as long as I've remembered. At first, my recollections are blurred images beginning in 1937, when my parents and I had arrived home from India. They become sharper as I recollect the time of Mother's death and our moving in. They will end when the house is sold in 1951. It's as though the dining room were a vessel in which memories accumulated for years, piling up and spilling over.

As we begin our ritual Sunday dinner, it's a bright sunny day. I don't recall cloudy days, rainy days or snowy days. It is sunny. Grandpa carves a roast or disjoints a chicken, then passes the plate all the way down the table to Grandma. She adds potatoes and vegetables to the meat, passes a plate first to each of us three children, then to Dad and Grandpa. She serves herself last. In her Sunday two-piece dress (no aprons worn at the table), and white hair piled on top of her head (to cover a bald spot), Grandma Clara Dickey Parsons keeps an eye on our plates. It's important that we be well nourished. We don't leave food on our plates, for we would hear again a concern about starving children in China or Armenia.

Grandpa is the major actor at dinnertime, but Grandma presides with subtle grace, attending to our manners as well as our balanced diets. "Always break your bread before buttering," she had instructed, "and since it's not nice to correct someone in public, let's work out a secret code, shall we?" Once in a while during our meals we hear her say "BYBBB," with a laugh-light in her eye. Both Grandpa and Dad seem indulgent, so either they know the secret code or are familiar with her ways.

While upholding these dinnertime rules and rituals, Grandma also makes space for Grandpa to shine, but doesn't forget to include everyone with an observation or question. Today we'd call her a facilitator. A new visitor wouldn't conclude, however, that Grandma also gave speeches in the cause of peace. Nor would the guest know that she wrote well, had worked with contractors to build nine houses, and could surprise us with her playfulness. Grandma shares her own accomplishments at other times. At dinner, she serves others.

Grandpa is six feet tall and stout. He doesn't look overweight, for his double-breasted suit is forgiving. He parts his white hair on the left, sits straight, and happily surveys the table with his one blue eye. The other eye, blinded and whitened in a shooting accident years before, seems fixed on a different horizon. The ring finger of one hand had been shortened at the top knuckle by a misdirected ax – an accident that might have occurred while beginning a home, garden, and orchard on their original three and one-half acres.

Although my recollections of these meals have coalesced into one image, there were many dinnertime gatherings, all unfolding in comfortable rhythm. Abundant food and longer conversations marked Sunday dinners. The main course usually required slow cooking: pot roast or chicken stew, started well before we began the three-block walk to church. Grandma trusted the stove's reliability and her own sense of timing. When we returned from church, she added dumplings to the stew or made gravy for the meat.

By the time for apple pie – made with apples collected in the small backyard orchard and served with cheddar cheese in the English manner – the conversation became lively. Perhaps the properly made British tea stimulated both the conversation and Grandpa's faint English accent. (His family had immigrated when he was a child.) "There was another lynching in the South," my grandfather once said to the other adults, who somehow knew, all of them nodding their heads with sorrow. "Roosevelt should take action," Grandpa would insist. "He can't," my father might say, always analytical, "he needs the Dixie votes, his hands are tied, he's onto the war effort." Then my grandmother might chime in "What about Mrs. Roosevelt? She could speak out or find a way to do something."

Grandpa's seated bounce conveyed his enthusiasm for conversation and stories. It might be about Henry Wallace's progressive agricultural policies – he had been Secretary of Agriculture under President Franklin Delano Roosevelt. Grandpa could be outraged when discussing any kind of injustice, as in this excerpt from his regular "Parsonalities" column, published for nearly twenty years in *The Hennepin County Review,* the newspaper in neighboring Hopkins.

No Empire

Churchill's declaration that he did not take office to liquidate the British Empire was clap-trap, very silly and very damaging to the allied cause. He ought to know that the British Empire ceased to exist, save as a ghost of itself, after the First World War. And, he should know that the ghost is gradually thinning out into mere air. It is no disrespect to our ally to declare that we, the people of the United States, are not going to sacrifice our boys to insure the fat old Tories of Great Britain a continuation of their privileges based on the rape of India. Wendell Willkie never did as much service to his country as when he declared that we cannot face the nations of the Pacific until we have made clear to them that we do not believe in empire.[3]

Because Dad had taught school for six and one-half years in India, he must have cited events in that country as examples of empire, oppression, and injustice. It isn't hard for me to think of Grandpa's anger and Dad's distress in connection with the 1944 famine in Bengal, when millions died in spite of a plentiful crop. "Three million," Dad said, "three million," as he looked at his lap while shaking his head. It was said that the British Army took the grain for their troops.

When the subject of the Imperial British in India came up at the table, my father hunched forward, eager to tell another story. "You know how the British love their scotch and soda? Well in the hill station near the school where we lived, there was hardly any ice available. For a long time it had been shipped over from Belmont, Massachusetts, to Bombay [now Mumbai]." (Fresh-water springs feed Belmont's lake in Massachusetts – today, one can purchase bottled water labeled "Belmont Springs.") This lake was a source of ice for a wide area, including India, amazing as that now seems to me. Inside the ships, the huge blocks of ice were insulated in sawdust. From Bombay it was some distance to New Delhi, and then another day's train trip landed the ice in Dehra Dun. "After that," Dad said, "it could take most of another day to get up the foothills to Mussoorie by cart. Naturally, the ice had now shrunk and couldn't last the summer. So one hotel owner concocted a plan."

Dad's eyes got brighter as he referred to a hole in the mountain rock behind the hotel – perhaps it had been enlarged with coolie pickaxes. Then he completed the story: "During the winter after a snowfall, the coolies would jump in with their bare feet and pack down the snow, forming ice. They did this all winter long, and when summer came the British gathered in the lounge to enjoy their scotch and soda." Not aware (I thought, when hearing this story again as an adult) that the bare brown feet of a despised people had formed ice for their drinks.

When hearing these stories, I wasn't aware that Grandpa was directing the conversation. Now I think he was like a schoolmaster who loved to raise issues, hear others' thoughts, and examine positions from this angle or that. He said as much in "Parsonalities."

Conversation

Some people seem to think that conversation is disputation or personalities or gossip or a monologue. But it is none of these, although each has its distinct place in our social system. For instance, disputation or argument is a good game – as good as bridge, if the players observe the rules – never to let personal emotion enter the game or try to prove a case by an isolated instance or two. But at its best, it is not conversation.[4]

A Companionship

What then is conversation? It is the comradeship of two or more – but not many more – through a forest of ideas. They stop here and there, as they would in a real forest, to examine this phenomenon or that. They may even pull an idea to pieces and they will change their direction many times in the course of an hour.[5]

Sometimes the teapot ran out as Sunday dinnertime conversations wandered and became livelier. "Is there any more tea?" someone would ask, so Grandma would leave the table to boil more water, add it to the leaves, allow it to steep, and pour another cup. The talk continued then, and affects me now.

Holiday and Sunday dinners represent, to me, the essence of home. Those meals formed the ground for my adult conviction – my conscious Christian conviction – that those who eat together are formed into community. In this community, positive values are held to the light, but family secrets are also pushed into darkness. My grandparents were committed Christians, active in the church they – and Great-Grandfather – had helped found: Edina Morningside Community Church, UCC. It's the church where I was confirmed, the church that holds the progressive tradition forming our views of a society that cares for "the widow, the orphan, and the stranger." Sunday meals had a sacred quality, seamless with Sunday worship, church potlucks and Holy Communion. In all these rituals we become bound together as we hear the stories of the tradition, consume them, make them a part of ourselves, and access the sacred dimension of human community. The conversations of those years echo today, whenever my family gathers for a meal.

CHAPTER 4

Things Get Rearranged

———

AFTER MOTHER DIED, WE MOVED into our grandparents' home in the Village of Morningside, the Minneapolis suburb where they had pioneered. Dad must have overseen the house sale, the packing, the loading, and the moving, all of which I've forgotten. We three children were already settling in. Grandma and Grandpa's welcome seems seamless now. How could it have been? It required reorganizing their home.

They had done this in the past. References to boarders pop up throughout their letters of the nineteen-thirties. Since they had three bedrooms, an unoccupied room could be let out, providing welcome income for our grandparents' Depression Era finances. When Dad had taught school in Aitken, Minnesota, and later moved to India, a boarder settled into one of the rooms. Ernest, Dad's younger brother, had the third room throughout his junior and senior high school years – the mid-sized room, I imagine.

When Grandma and Grandpa reorganized in 1944, they put Dad into the smallest bedroom, to the left of the upstairs landing. Other people might have put stenciling or a wallpaper strip just beneath the ceiling. But Dad posted *Time* magazine covers. He'd been one of the beginning subscribers, and covers from that first edition, up until the latest printing, ran around the wall. Famous people regarded him as he sat at his desk correcting high school science and math papers.

Carol, Dudley, and I filled the mid-sized corner room, which boasted brand-new bunk beds. Since Carol and I both wanted the top one, we switched off each week. Dudley had a single bed in the same room. A window overlooked the back yard with its elm and weeping willow trees, lawn, orchard, and vegetable garden. Grandma and Grandpa continued to use the largest room until a new one, with its own half-bath, could be built over the basement-level garage.

To build the addition, Grandpa had to petition the War Production Board to allow an early conversion from coal to gas heat. The furnace would have to be expanded in any case, so the Board granted permission even though the war was still going on. I don't know when the new room was begun, but it's a safe guess – given Minnesota winters – that it was completed during the summer of 1945. Probably the sale of 304 E. 48th Street helped provide money for the addition. The niche next to the dining room, which had held Grandma's tea caddy and a few treasured dishes, became the access point for a new passageway. Three steps and a doorway led into the new blue bedroom for Grandma and Grandpa.

Then we rearranged our rooms again. Dad, Carol, Dudley, and I could spread out.

None of this changing-about could have been easy for our grandparents. At least, I would find it difficult to take in my entire family at this time in my life. Yet, it seems to have been treated as "something one does." Support Groups didn't exist – although the church was always a community of support. I imagine neighbors, friends, and family asked quiet questions and made affirmations. We three children accepted the new arrangement without wondering; at least, I don't recall questions, doubts, or worries. I know that Dad was involved in the transition, but he was working, and

Grandma was home full time. I'm sure we were stunned, but we knew we were cared for.

The entire event – our mother's death, our moving in, and a household's adjustment – merited one small paragraph in "Parsonalities," where I now see hints about challenges.

Life Begins at Sixty-five

Our grandchildren are with us – "to love, honor and obey." They call us back from retirement to the busy world. They have pertinent questions for us to answer such as "Where is God? What does 'futility' mean? What does a squirrel act so jiggly for? How does corn grow?' They already have friends who help also to fill our lives and problems for us to solve. We have to grow or make our home a mausoleum for these bright young Americans. And so we make our choice on the side of life. Anyhow, what are years but man-made measures?[6]

Grandma took the lead in easing us into our new home. She escorted us to Morningside Elementary School just around the corner on 42nd Street, to register for the school year. I was going to enter grade five, and Carol grade two. The building is still there, now a Montessori School. Because Morningside had no kindergarten, Dudley rode a bus to Wooddale School in the contiguous town, Edina.

We became part of the Edina-Morningside Community Congregational Church. Grandpa's stories reminded us that he and his father had been leaders in gathering this church. Early church meetings had taken place on Morningside Road in a sixteen by twenty-four foot chapel. It still stands, converted into a home. Church members, including Great-Grandfather Henry William Parsons, built it themselves. When the congregation grew, leaders built a new stucco and timbered building a block further up Morningside Road. In the late forties, the building was expanded, altered, and faced with stone.

Besides Sunday School each week, the church sponsored such groups as Girl Scouts for me, and Campfire Girls for Carol. One year the church held a fair to raise money, and my proper Grandma dressed up as a Gypsy woman. She chattered away to me as she put together her outfit. "Shall I wear this skirt, or this other one, do you think?" The result was a gold-patterned turban wound around her head, a printed top, and a long flowered skirt – a deliberate mismatch of patterns. She completed her costume with a bold application of rouge and bright lipstick. After we arrived at church for the event, she disappeared into the women's room to change, and then emerged to take her place within a tent-like space comprised of material draped over supports. Or maybe Dad set up his WWII surplus army tent that we used for camping. Inside, Gypsy Grandma sat near a low table set with a lighted candle, where she read tealeaves for church members. Because she knew everyone, a gracious subtlety would have been the only trick to the readings.

In addition to organized church events, school, and weekly trips to the library for our reading habits, daily unsupervised play was a given. The neighborhood was safe – it still is – and I didn't roam far. There was a marsh near 42nd Street and France Avenue, the residue of an ancient lakebed, which consisted of spongy mounds rising from shallow swamp water. A friend dared me to explore this with her. Danger thrilled us as we jumped from one of these hillocks to another. But my shoe got caught and was sucked into a watery hole. The adults didn't seem upset when I arrived home in one wet sock and one shoe – they simply asked how it happened. No one said, "Don't do that again," but I didn't return to that "playground."

The vacant lot behind the house was closer. There was a slope to this lot, trees were crowded together, and vines climbed the trunks and branches. Perhaps they were wild grapevines, for they were heavy and strong enough to bear our weight as we swung on them, starting from high ground, then leaping off the vine onto the humus-y floor. We were fighting the Japanese.

I'm amazed at the ways our grandparents provided new life for us. There were structure and liveliness, connections with others in neighborhood and church, accommodation to changing needs, recreation, and work. We didn't talk about Mother's death, but the adults worked hard to provide us with a safe space in which we could grow and flourish. The nurturing daily mealtimes epitomize their caring: a well-set table, attention to manners, and lively conversation. The lasting impact of table rituals continues as an expectation when I prepare meals for my own family, when I want to foster connections and nurture identity. It continues as a longing when my family says "Let's just have buffet for Thanksgiving." In my heart, family members always sit around a table, eat together, and tell stories. And those missing are always present.

CHAPTER 5

The Saturday Lunch Club

———

GRANDMA GUIDED THE FLOW OF dinnertime conversation and stories, but Grandpa's opinions and declarations dominated. No one raised voices in their household, but sometimes Grandpa's words carried little drops of spittle, so passionate was he, so forceful his ideas. Surely the adults disagreed about analysis, or tactics, or political leaders, but much of the substance has escaped me. It's the liveliness, the tempo, the open quality I recall. It still feels zesty.

Saturday Lunch Club discussions often became the starting point for table talk. This club had been founded in 1906 as a forum for free discussion, and my grandparents were early members. They both shared opinions freely while we lived with them. But later, as the Cold War developed, their progressive ideas became problematic to some family members and friends. When the McCarthy Era took hold, anyone with "leftist" views was suspected of being a Communist, subversive, and un-American. When an adult, I recognized the mood change, which had taken place in our family after Dad re-married in 1947. My curiosity about the Saturday Lunch Club revived. I was due for a regular visit to Minnesota, learned that the Minneapolis Public Library held Saturday Lunch Club archives, and made an appointment to see the collection.

On a sunny day in May 2005, I walked into the new Library building, glanced at a posted directory, and rose in the glass-enclosed
elevator to the floor for the Archive Room. I stopped at the desk,
identified myself, and found a seat at one of the long tables. High
windows filtered the light. A young librarian wheeled out a grey,
two-tiered cart holding several boxes of papers.

I leafed through folders. They contained newspaper clippings,
a pamphlet about the Liberal movement my grandfather had co-
authored, and a history of the Club. There were Depression Era
letters from Grandpa, begging members to pay their dues: "Send a
dollar bill, money order, check, or as Sears once said, 'Send something that looks like money.'" And there was a set of reminder postcards announcing meeting plans. It looked as though these archives
consisted entirely of Grandpa's papers. I didn't see other sources.

I became anxious. I hadn't expected so much material when
I'd made the appointment, and the room was scheduled to be
open for only two hours during my Twin Cities stay. Even so, there
was enough time to be astonished at the story disclosed by the
fifty-year record of speakers. These were the political and social
luminaries of the early twentieth century Progressive movement. I
had to make a list. William Jennings Bryan was one presenter – a
candidate for President three times, peace activist, and winner of
the Scopes "Monkey Trial" debate in 1925. Clarence Darrow, who
took the other side in that trial, also spoke to the club. The muck-
raking journalist Lincoln Steffens was yet another. He had visited
the Soviet Union in 1919 and developed a brief infatuation with
Communism ("I have been over into the future and it works!" he
wrote in 1921). Margaret Sanger, birth control advocate, Socialist
and founder of Planned Parenthood is on the list. So is Upton
Sinclair, the Socialist who wrote 90 books and received the Pulitzer
Prize in 1942.

Members heard speeches about political, economic, World War
II, and postwar developments in countries throughout the world.

Often the presenters had traveled or lived in those places, and gave first-hand observations. Domestic issues, such as wages, trade, and the banking system didn't escape attention. Discussion topics about making and keeping the peace are scattered throughout the Club's programs from its beginning.

This roster exemplified the stated purpose of the Club: to be open for the purpose of free debate on political, social, and economic issues. And debate there was – not always civil. A news story described a meeting, which took place early in 1939.

Soviet Speaker Here Challenged by Woman

Anna Strong, Moscow Editor, Accused of 'Lying' About Russia

A woman in the audience yesterday upset a meeting of the Saturday Lunch Club with shouts of "Shame! Shame, you traitors!" after a talk by Anna Louis Strong, American-born editor of the Moscow Daily News, in which Miss Strong traced the progress of the Soviet Union in its five-year plans for industrial independence.

The woman jumped to her feet at conclusion of the talk and shouted: "Madame Speaker, you have painted a rosy picture of Russia. Now, how about the other side – the liquidation of the farms and the treatment of the poor peasants? How about them, Madame Speaker?"

After another exchange with the speaker, the chairman of the meeting – who was Grandpa – attempted to calm the woman, as did another participant:

Again [the questioner] jumped to her feet, furious, and pushed the other woman back into her chair.

From the audience came cries of "Take her out!"

A man near the rear of the hall stood up. "What's become of General Bluecher, Miss Strong?"

And the woman added, "And the poor peasants, Madame speaker?" A policeman was summoned and the woman hurried from the hall. [7]

Grandpa was conducting that meeting because he was taking his turn. Members didn't want the Club to become hardened into an institution, so there were no permanent officers. There was an Executive Committee, which met to select speakers, address the ever-present issue of finances, and find space for gatherings. The founders wanted debate to be in "the English style," in which members feel free to heckle a speaker, or groan with displeasure. As I glanced through papers in the folder, I saw reports indicating that most meetings were milder than the Anna Louise Strong discussion, but lively nonetheless, according to a report in *The Minneapolis Tribune*:

Kline, Humphrey Join in Debate
Mayor Marvin L. Kline and Hubert Humphrey spoke from the same platform for the first time during the mayoralty campaign.... Both candidates appeared before the Saturday Lunch Club, an organization which has the reputation of being able to grill speakers to the squirming point during its weekly sessions at Miller's Cafeteria.[8]

Reading these items reminded me that I'd attended the Saturday Lunch Club, probably after we moved into our grandparents' home. That's when I became aware of Grandpa's political interests. He wanted me to have first-hand experience of the Club's lively discussions.

I sat next to him on the yellow streetcar's shiny wicker bench as it carried us on tracks along France Avenue, fed by its stiff cable attached to the overhead wire. We turned east to move onto the right-of-way beside Lake Calhoun, and then connected with Hennepin

Avenue. Soon we passed the large United Methodist Church at the bend – Grandpa often explained that Hennepin had once been a cow path and "cows don't walk a straight line." (Sometimes he said the bend was there because the street's contours followed a former Indian trail.) I would have dressed myself in "good" clothing, for Grandpa wanted to show me off, a reluctant guest, to his debating friends and colleagues. As the streetcar clacked toward downtown Minneapolis, he spat on his clean linen handkerchief and wiped a dirty spot off my face. This scrub-up method wasn't unusual, and I hated it.

I was heading toward eleven years of age and adjusting to a new home, so I couldn't appreciate Grandpa's stance on the issues he debated through forums, letters, phone calls, sidewalk conversations, and committee leadership. Although I'd known about the Saturday Lunch Club because it was part of dinnertime talk, I didn't understand its significance at the time of my visit with my grandfather. (It was a recognized institution in the Twin Cities, a "second university" after the University of Minnesota – according to a popular saying.)

After leaving the streetcar, we entered the meeting room. Grandpa seated me at a round table with white cloth, napkins, tableware, and water glasses. While I waited for food, he introduced me to old-looking men. I ate my lunch and endured the business meeting, presentation, and debate, which I don't remember.

Now I would love to time-travel, observe, and listen. I want to hear Grandpa's provocative remarks. I'm sure he enjoyed firing up discussion and arguing with responses. He had reported one meeting in a 1931 letter to my father, who was then in India:

Dear Dudley,
        I have just returned from the Saturday Lunch Club meeting which was addressed by Chas. Keyes on the proposed repeal of

a franchise granting a 20 year lease of our new coal dock to a private coal company. I incurred some hostility from some of these with whom I have broken bread for years, on account of my favoring the retention of the franchise....

But, I probably shall not be put into the class of reactionaries by most people. I adduced to my argument the illustration of "the greatest genius of this past fifty years, Nicolai Lenin, a passionate lover of the principle who suffered Siberian exile and vile imprisonment for his views but who was strategist enough to permit the New Economic Policy until Bolshevism was strong enough to go forward in its vital form, and who then struck the concession to capitalism from his program." [9]

Maybe Grandpa didn't understand the significance of the brief New Economic Policy. This policy had permitted individuals to augment their income by selling handcrafts or garden produce. It was a practice that sustained urban and rural poor. However, some individuals (called NEP-men) made high profits through re-sales. Those who augmented their income were barely tolerated at first, and then persecuted. Stalin destroyed the policy in 1928 (not Lenin, as Grandpa says in his letter). I don't want to think that Grandpa agreed with the muckraker Lincoln Steffens, who saw the retraction of the policy as brutal but necessary. Yet his letter to Dad forces me to recognize that he did agree with Steffens – at least, in 1931. At that time, discussion abounded – certainly in the Saturday Lunch Club – about the new society in the USSR. Speakers who'd visited or lived in Russia were featured once or twice a year from 1931 to 1947. Grandpa saw Russia as full of promise – as he did any proposal for economic equality. But he was seeing a different horizon, from that which I knew later in my college years during the Cold War, when suspicion and fear of "Reds" prevailed.

Because the Club was chartered for open discussion, members must have expressed strong feelings about the many topics – the co-operative movement, prison reform, and recognition of Russia were just a few. Hubert Humphrey was a member early in his political career, but became less active. He belonged to the right wing of the Democratic-Farmer Labor Party, whereas the left wing supported Henry Wallace and his followers.

Each summer, Club members left restaurant settings to enjoy a picnic. My grandparents hosted several of these in their backyard – Grandpa wrote about one of them in "Parsonalities:"

Notes on a Picnic

Last week I had something to say about that great American institution – the picnic. This week I want to dwell on a particular picnic – in our backyard on Saturday, July 11th. It was the annual outing of the Saturday Lunch Club, "now in its thirty-fourth year of town hall democracy" as its letterhead properly proclaims. A hundred and twenty members participated in the festivities – 3 doctors, 4 lawyers, 3 clergymen, 12 public school teachers, 2 college professors, 10 "civil servants," as the English would say, 10 business men, 10 office and store employees, 3 manual workers and their wives, sisters and several children. They were Republicans, Democrats, Farmer-Laborites, Catholics, Protestants, Jews, conservatives and liberals – a good cross-section of the America we love and cherish.[10]

Speakers that day included "Mr. Humphrey, the candidate for the Farmer-Labor nomination in the 3rd District..."

I think about these meetings, their topics of discussion and debate, the Club's founding purpose, my grandfather's lively mind and his enthusiasm for meeting (and instructing) others. They exemplified citizen participation, discovery, and a willingness to explore contentious matters. I feel proud that my family participated. Even so, I was surprised to find in the archives a 1948 letter from John A. Blatnik, Representative to Congress from Minnesota. The Cold War had begun, and Grandpa had invited the Ambassador from Socialist Yugoslavia to speak in the backyard of 4210 Alden Drive.

Dear Mr. Parsons:

In answer to your card of June 18, I have just checked with the Yugoslav Embassy, and was told that the Ambassador had written you a few days ago, accepting your invitation to speak at your picnic on July 10.

The Ambassador is very happy to have this opportunity to speak to the Saturday Lunch Club picnic, and is certain he will be there. Only some extraordinary situation or emergency at the last moment, which he does not anticipate, will force him to change his plans....

With best wishes for a successful picnic, and warmest personal regards,

Very sincerely yours,
(signed) John A. Blatnik, M.C.[11]

It seems that letters had crossed in the mail. But this one also contains some "wiggle-room" should the Ambassador think it imprudent to arrive at my grandparents' house. As it turned out, a substitute spoke on July 7th, on the topic "Who Are the Slavs – and What?"

Whatever prompted Grandpa to invite an Ambassador from the Soviet bloc to a picnic in his backyard? Was it too early in the Cold War for him to be sensitive to those political tensions? Was he always blind to them? Did these tensions count for little within his giant framework of peace and justice? Was it his enthusiastic pushing for debate? Was the idea generated within the executive committee of the Club? Grandpa wasn't the only person to hold progressive views.

Although I'll never know his reasoning, I'm coming to see him as committed to an overarching dream for peace, economic equality, and social justice in the world. And to that end he consistently engaged in interactions with others: letters, debate, instruction, conversation, and speeches. While I wouldn't have the courage to offer an invitation like that, I want to be there to cheer him on.

Today it's hard to grasp the nineteen-thirties' atmosphere of Midwest Populism, Progressivism, widespread interest in Socialism, the ferment of debate and argument, and the heritage of justice-loving Christians. All these influenced my grandparents. Their letters bring their perspective to life, and now my ears become quickly attuned to news stories and memoirs of the time. It's hard to enter the past without blaming it for lacking the present perspective, as Mary Luti had suggested. But in this case my present perspective resonates with that of my grandparents'. I might not embrace it wholly, but I envy their opportunity for vigorous debate fostered in the Saturday Lunch Club.

Bit by bit, I patch together my understanding.

CHAPTER 6

Grandpa's Rules for Reading

———

GRANDPA SNAGGED ME AT THE bottom of the stairs: "Here! Stand here!" He pointed to a spot on the living room carpet, and stood opposite me. I looked up at him. "Move closer." I moved. It felt too close. "Did you read the book?"

"Yes."

"Well, then, what did you think of it?"

"It was go-o-o-d." I looked at my feet, toes on the line where he'd ordered me to stand.

On November 7, 1944, he had presented me with a copy of *Ivanhoe* by Sir Walter Scott – he knew I loved to read. "It's my birthday," he announced, "and on my birthday I like to give books away. Here's a great story for you, and when it's your birthday you'll give me a book report. Agreed?" I nodded. And now it was Judgment Day, my own birthday seven weeks later, ample time to have read the classic set in an era long before the day I turned ten.

I had not read the book.

I *had* read – and forgotten – the first sentence, which says, "In that pleasant district of merry England which is watered by the river Don there extended in ancient times a large forest covering the greater part of the hills and valleys which lie between Sheffield and the pleasant town of Doncaster."[12]

Then I put the book on my shelf, found other things to do, other books to read. I kept delaying *Ivanhoe* whenever I became conscious of Grandpa's plan.

Now it was exam time. "What were the names of some of the towns in England?" I rifled through my brain, empty of merry towns. I was silent, knowing that Grandpa knew, and I knew that he knew I had lied.

I waited for the thunderhead to let go. What would happen? Extra duty with dinner dishes? My father informed? An order to "try again and do it right this time?" Instead, "You may go," with – maybe – a small smile. Released from my spot on the carpet, I climbed the stairs to hide in my room. I opened the book and discovered the answer to his question. It was in the first sentence.

I never did get around to reading "Ivanhoe."

But the frontispiece (was it one of N.C. Wyeth's?) is vivid right now: a red streak flashes across the picture. It belongs to a pennant; a knight rides a rearing horse; they are silhouetted against a grey sky. A thunderhead dominates the sky, and a stream of light slices through the cloud. The light could symbolize the hero's promise. But the cloud represents my fears on that quiz day.

I don't believe that Grandpa usually gave away books on his own birthday – that one time was a try-out of his delicious idea. But, in spite of Sir Walter Scott, both Grandma and Grandpa fostered my love of reading. How could they not? They were examples. They were always reading. They talked about books. They passed books back and forth with Dad, with friends, and with each other. Grandfather often burst into the house gesturing with a library book, excited to be the first borrower: "Duveen! Here's the new book about Duveen!" (Duveen was an influential art dealer, and Grandpa seemed to be interested in everything.)

When we lived with our grandparents for those three years, we used the village library, a short walk away. But in more prosperous years, family members had purchased books, for down in the basement a narrow room held a wall of shelves filled with old volumes. The bookcase butted the high windows opening onto the garden. At the far end, a door gave access to the back yard. We used the room as a corridor, and I often stopped to browse. I was attracted to *The Stars in Their Courses* by Jeans, written in 1931, even though I knew it was out of date – he used the archaic spelling "shew" for "show." Yet I was drawn in by the description of atmosphere, nebulae and asteroids. I read it standing up. I also read, on my feet, Paul de Kruif's *The Microbe Hunters*, written around 1926.

Grandpa's social concerns, of course, shaped his recommendations. "Have you read Zola's *Germinal*?" he once asked me. At another time he gave me a copy of Eliot's *The Mill on the Floss*. I didn't get past the first page of Eliot's novel, either. The idea of age-appropriate literature didn't govern his suggestions. Or maybe he thought these *were* age-appropriate, and that I would love Sir Walter Scott, George Eliot, and Emile Zola before my twelfth year.

I did read *Water Babies*, by Charles Kingsley, a Victorian clergyman who belonged to the Christian Socialist movement in England. (I suppose this movement had influenced Grandpa's father.) A main character was a poor chimney sweep, who died and became a water baby – a kind of soul that lived on underwater and swam to another shore, as I recall. Grandpa's interest might have been the chimney sweep's poverty, but the swimming water baby comforted me about my mother's death. Even though I didn't feel my mother's presence, I understood the story to mean that something of a dead person survives – somewhere, somehow.

Little Women was another source of comfort. Grandma encouraged me to read stories of strong women, and I became involved in the March family. As I sat on the living room couch, crying when Beth died, Grandma came in from the kitchen, put her face against mine, and cried with me. Her sadness must have included tears for her stillborn daughter, who had been delivered in between two of her sons – I don't know which ones. "I had a baby girl once," Grandma had told me. "But she was born dead. I wanted to name her Jeanette, after my mother." Tears brimmed over for Beth, for my mother, and for Uncle Ernest, who had died before he was twenty. Beth's death helped me to grieve. I still turn to books when facing inevitable losses of living: children who grow up too fast, friends who move away, divorces in the family, deaths. Because of my grandparents, books are friends and allies for the current time, as well as doorways into other ages and worlds.

Grandpa insisted we treat books with respect: "Never turn down the corner of a page," he said. "If you can't remember where you left off, then you weren't reading carefully." He gave his rules for reading in short spurts, turning away to make a phone call, head for the garden, or enter the kitchen. "Do you know how to open a new book?" We were standing in the living room after one of his library trips. "Never crack the spine – that just ruins it. Open a few pages at a time, press down gently, then add a few more pages, pressing down, until you've opened the entire book." Another time: "Never eat while you're reading. Crumbs will fall on the page and stain it. That's a terrible thing to do to a book." I didn't mind Grandpa's admonishments because I knew he'd grown up in a poor household where his parents valued and encouraged education.

When I became a senior in high school, though, an English teacher challenged me. This was when I was passing myself off as a sophisticate, carrying around Proust's *Swann's Way*. My teacher was leaning against a doorjamb just before class. "Janet, have you ever read Mickey Spillane?" I had read the mystery writer, but didn't expect that question. "Your grandfather has too much influence," she said. "Try something different." I nodded and walked past her to take my seat in the classroom. But I couldn't shuck Grandpa's impact.

I still practice some of his rules. I open new books carefully and always use a bookmark. I dislike seeing a turned down page in a library book. I do read while eating. But I never, ever drop food on the page – that's what I claim.

In my home a small shelf holds five thin books that my grandfather authored. All are about Minnesota history, and at least two were used in the Minneapolis school system. My favorite is *Heroes of the Northwest*.

I recently opened its maroon cover and turned to the preface, which reminded me that these sixteen stories about pioneers were intended for ten-year-olds, to sustain "their interest in the lives of men without [promoting] militarism." Then I read all the biographical sketches, curious about the heroes selected. These included Dr. William Worrell Mayo, of the Mayo Clinic; Little Crow, one of three American Indians featured; and James J. Hill, the railroad builder. I was charmed by a moralistic quality not obvious in today's textbooks:

> History calls the whites who came to America settlers; to the Indians they were conquerors. The whites looked upon the lands of the Indians, whether or not these lands were prairie or covered with timber, as wasted...They did not understand that an Indian cornfield or garden was as precious in the eyes of its cultivator as is a white man's valuable to him.... One of the most sorrowful figures among the many chiefs who were forced off their lands was Black Hawk.[13]

I noted that most sketches begin with the hero's boyhood, probably intended to hook a ten-year-old. There might be no *theme of militarism*, but there's enough conflict and action to capture attention: the Civil War, Indian massacres, betrayals, rivers and snowstorms impeding pioneer journeys. I smiled as I read Grandpa's framing a moment of personal revenge as honor and courage: John Lind, a Governor of Minnesota, had the dignity to wait until *after* he retired from public office, and *then* assaulted a man who had insulted him. I love it all. I love descriptions of leaders who borrowed money, worked hard, expanded business, grew fortunes. My progressive grandfather wrote with enthusiasm about capitalists, for he thought some made it possible for many to benefit from America's wealth. And he wanted *Heroes of the Northwest* to inspire ten-year-olds to live nobly.

I closed the book with an idea: I would give it a severe test. "Dylan," I asked my nine-year-old grandson, "I'd like your help. I want your opinion about something. Would you please read this chapter, and tell me what you think of it?" I showed him a short piece on Black Hawk.

"But it's long!" (Dylan was reading constantly, books of all lengths, in English and in Russian.)

"It's only nine pages."

"I'll read the first page." This was not young Janet nodding agreement and making false promises about "Ivanhoe."

I bargained with him until we agreed on three pages, which he quickly read.

"I already know this about white people betraying Indians. In my opinion, this chapter is in the middle: some kids would like it, some wouldn't. Some words are hard, like 'consequently.' But it's not very interesting because I already know it." He spoke in his polite voice: quiet and effective in deflating my own delicious idea that Dylan might learn directly from his Great-Great Grandfather.

But I was happy. Grandpa would have been pleased that attitudes toward American Indians had changed, and proud that his Great-Great Grandson knew it. And Dylan's response did come from a moral perspective, although his school material might not have put it as those chapters did, in *Heroes of the Northwest.*

CHAPTER 7
Campfire, Fish, and Potatoes

———

I LOVE SKUNK SCENT. To me, it's not an odor. It's a scent. Whenever I cross a skunk's trail, a whiff summons the memory of a road in Wisconsin.

Dad is driving the car. I'm in the front passenger seat; Dudley and Carol are in the back. We are sleepy and quiet. Rain has stopped, but clouds cover the night sky, so we can't see stars through the windows. Our headlights shine on wet pavement and sweep along fir trees. We pass a skunk's trail, and its perfume reaches us. I exclaim, "A skunk was here!" "Yes," says Dad. At some point he turns the car around and we head back to our tent for the night.

He'd resorted to the car ride after a rainy afternoon at our campsite on Lake Staples. We'd stayed cross-legged on sleeping bags in the tent, but ran out of card games. Soon the three of us were bored, irritable, and annoying. Dad had no more ideas for diversion until he thought of a nighttime car ride. I smile now when I realize that Dad's attempt to deal with our bad moods resulted in my associating skunk scent with warmth, comfort, and swishing wheels on a road.

That ride had occurred on our second trip, after we had bought a car. Transportation for our first expedition wasn't so simple, because we took a train. This trek probably occurred in 1945, when I was ten, Carol eight, and Dudley six. It was a year after our move into Grandma and Grandpa's home, while Dad was still coping with his new role as a single parent. Camping was a good way to be together – and the only affordable vacation. Our destination was our family's strip of land, situated between Lake Staples and a swamp. There was enough room on this site for a WWII surplus tent, a clump of birches, a campfire pit, a clothesline, and five million mosquitos.

We needed to carry all our equipment, but Dad was an experienced camper, and knew how to manage. The tent and its stakes were one heavy roll. Each of us carried a sleeping bag. Our clothing must have been rolled inside these, for we didn't need much besides bathing suits, jeans, sweaters, and warm pajamas. A metal box contained cooking and eating utensils, matches, and staples such as flour, sugar, and coffee. Surely we didn't take streetcars to the train station in downtown Minneapolis. A neighbor might have given us a ride, or perhaps we called a taxi.

In the station, we boarded a train with tickets for Danbury, Wisconsin, located in the northern part of the state. The area was filled with summer cabins situated on lakes abounding with fish. The forest, threaded with red clay roads, harbored deer targeted during hunting season. Indian reservations were nearby.

When the train pulled into Danbury, we all descended with our bundles. Perhaps there was a depot, but Dad told us to wait on the platform with our luggage while he walked into town, to find someone willing to drive us to the lake. After he returned with a driver and loaded us into the car, we stopped at a small grocery store to buy fresh food. With hamburger meat, hot dogs, buns, milk and eggs, we headed for the campsite. Dad was confident we could catch fish and pick blueberries to go along with these basics for the five days ahead.

He knew the way. Before the Depression, Grandpa had purchased seven lots on Lake Staples. He dreamed of developing these into a resort to be called "Parsons Lake Park." When that idea fizzled, Grandpa planned to leave one lot to each of his children, and sell the rest. Dad kept his for a while, but the economy, costs of re-settling after living in India, and the drain of Mother's illness meant that Dad couldn't pay taxes. He lost his land. The other lots were also forfeited because of taxes, except for the one strip between lake and swamp. This became our family campground, and we loved it.

To reach it, Dad directed the driver off the main road and onto a two-track lane. The ruts were so deep that he had to maneuver along the rut sides to avoid scraping the undercarriage on the middle ridge. He parked the car, we unloaded, and Dad asked the driver to return on the morning of the fifth day.

Dad had always been an enthusiastic tenter. He camped while growing up and did so in India as leader of a Boy Scout troop. He loved to tell me about the morning when he awakened at a mountain site in India to see a man coming over the hill and approaching the camp. This was a British man, Dad stressed. He introduced himself, and ventured, "I wonder if you can help us. We're in a spot of trouble. The fact is – we're out of marmalade."

Since Dad loved to teach, he instructed us while setting up the tent, showed us how to hang clothesline from tree branches, and how to choose the best spot for our fire. We also had to select a place closer to the swamp for our toilet and degradable garbage. His next step was to borrow a boat for fishing – one came with a rental cabin on the next lot. Those renters were willing to loan the boat, and to let us use the sandy beach next to the dock. Now I realize Dad had made assumptions that worked out: he'd be able to get off a train and find a driver; he'd be able to borrow a rowboat; he could count on the driver's return on day five. He relied on neighborly attitudes. These assumptions seem risky, even crazy, today, but at the time people helped each other out. Danbury was a small town, and both the Depression and WWII were fresh experiences. People knew they needed each other.

After setting up the campsite, it must have been day's end and time to eat. I wonder if we lit a campfire, or if we ate sandwiches that first night. Although Dad never cooked in the kitchen at home, he liked to use a grill. He made coffee for himself. Was it in a percolator, or was it egg coffee? (Boil coffee grounds, remove pot from fire, add eggshells to coalesce and settle the grounds, and pour into a mug.) He made pancakes using tiny native blueberries, which we all picked from low bushes on nearby sunny slopes, or where sunlight fell through trees. He made chapattis, my favorite flatbread from India. He cleaned, scaled, and fried sunfish, which we caught with lines dropped over the boat side. We ate hamburgers and hot dogs. We added sweet corn purchased from a nearby farm within hiking distance. We finished evening meals by spearing marshmallows on green branches, and roasting them over the fire.

Cooking over a campfire sounds lovely, but it does involve work. We gathered dry wood, which had to be monitored once lighted, because the coals must be just right for cooking. While we ate, we heated water to be used for faces, hands, and dishes. Before washing pans, we scrubbed them with lakeshore sand. There might have been a pump on nearby property for drinking water, or it's possible we boiled lake water. Our baths were twice-daily swims.

Between meals, we splashed in the lake, went fishing, and sometimes hiked in the woods, always looking for blueberries. One day we came to a clearing where a dilapidated cabin stood. Dad went to the front door and knocked. No one answered. He pushed the door open, looked in, and beckoned us forward. Inside the room was a table with half-eaten food left in dishes. He explained that squatters were probably occupying the cabin, and disappeared when they heard us crashing through the woods. It was an early lesson that some people were so poor they had no place of their own. At the same time, I couldn't comprehend someone's claiming another person's cabin and moving in.

Each night as it became dusky we sat near the campfire, which discouraged mosquitoes. I don't know if we used repellents – DEET wasn't available for another decade. We listened to loons call in the twilight. When it was dark and clear, we saw stars everywhere. After we settled into our tent for sleep, Dad stayed up until the fire was safely out. Insect song and the scent of his pipe accompanied our drifting into sleep. When we awakened, we heard loons calling again.

After lunch on the fourth day, Dad called us together. "We have a problem to solve. We're running out of food. We ate it faster than I expected, and we didn't catch any fish yesterday or this morning. We're also short of money, Danbury is a long way off, and we have to pay the driver to take us to the train." As I listened, I was puzzled because everything had been so well organized.

Then Dad presented us with his plan. "There's a farm near here, and I noticed that the farmer grows potatoes. When it gets darker, I can go to the edge of the field and dig some up. No one will notice they're gone." I was slow to understand. My father was talking about stealing potatoes!

"Do all of you agree to this? The farmer won't miss a few. He's got a big field."

"No." I shook my head. "That's wrong."

Carol's eyes were on Dad. "That's stealing."

Dudley joined in. "No, we can't."

Dad looked at all of us. We were sober and certain. Dad looked accepting.

A bit later he asked us if we'd be all right if he left us alone for a while, but that we were not to go swimming. We stayed in the campground re-reading comic books, playing "Go Fish," and waiting.

When he returned, we lit the fire, boiled water, and ate our supper of corn on the cob and new potatoes. We didn't ask where he got the food. We assumed he'd bought it from the farmer. And I still don't know why he'd consulted with us.

Dad continued to camp all his life, into his eighties. I suppose he'd learned from his own parents. Grandpa had been on camping trips with his own family as a young man, but I don't recall my grandparents telling stories about expeditions or camping. It was Dad who developed an enthusiasm for it. He volunteered as a Scout Leader throughout his life, and took his children and grandchildren camping. My brothers Dudley, Rolf, and James benefitted the most. I didn't keep up the tradition, for I fancied myself a sophisticated city dweller. Now I regret that I didn't take my family camping during vacations, that we didn't toast marshmallows over a campfire, that we didn't hike together in woods slapping mosquitoes, that we didn't hear loons singing and laughing. I'm sad that my grandchildren Dylan and Jessica, Cian and Milo have never seen the Milky Way above a lake.

But there's hope: my older son Eric likes to camp. He, who lives in the middle of New York City, takes Cian on weekend trips. Soon he'll introduce Milo to the smell of fresh air and the whiff of a skunk's trail. Maybe the Milky Way will awe my grandchildren some day.

CHAPTER 8
Proper Clara

——

"GUESS WHAT! I'M WORKING ON taming a squirrel. Come on! It's just about time – he shows up every morning around eleven o'clock." It was a summer day when Grandma grabbed me, went to get a peanut or two, and drew me upstairs to a bedroom. It was the one that had become Dad's after the new room was built. She opened the window that overlooked the addition's slanted roof; it wasn't far from the elm that dominated one section of the backyard.

"We have to be quiet! You can't move or make a noise, or he won't come." She was putting peanuts on the sill. We stood still, waiting.

And then he arrived: small, reddish, flaps between legs providing transportation for this flying squirrel. He leaped from the elm tree; legs spread wide, gliding, gliding on the warm air until he landed. He picked up a peanut, sat there, twitched his tail, shelled the nut, ate it, grabbed the other one, tucked it into his cheek, ran down the roof with nails clicking, took off for land, and scampered up the elm. "Next I want to teach him to take it from my hand," said Grandma.

These occasional adventures surprised me, for Clara Dickey Parsons had routines. She and Grandpa observed Sunday as Sabbath, with a family meal and family time. She laundered on Monday, ironed on Tuesday, and spent Saturday cleaning and cooking so we wouldn't have to work on Sunday. She fine-tuned these routines for special occasions. She'd bring out the Havilland, with its tiny butter pats and crystal saltcellars with their minute glass spoons. She instructed me about proper placement of dinner plates, salad plates, glasses, silver, and napkins. She emphasized how lovely the table looked and how welcome guests would feel. I loved to set the table with her for those meals.

I don't know her schedule during school hours, but I'm sure there was one, which included a nap after lunch. After rising, she made herself a pot of tea, put the tray on the living room coffee table and enjoyed her perk-up. She sat there working on her current project, fingers holding and moving the fine cotton that became crocheted tablecloths to give at Christmas or birthdays. I see her sipping tea, then retrieving a Camel cigarette from an ashtray. It dangled from the corner of her mouth, her eyes narrowed against the smoke as she concentrated.

She must have timed her nap so that when we got home from school she'd be drinking her last sip, ready to greet us. She needed these habits to cope with our entrance into her home after our mother died – it must have been a challenge to receive us when we were five, seven, and nine years of age, no matter how much she loved us. Although these habits were structured into her being, I think they were something else, as well. They provided a framework: they were like a vessel that could both contain and liberate her spontaneity. She was a proper lady whose love of life escaped its container and bubbled over.

Thus she was an ideal match for Grandpa. Her enthusiasms and openness to experience were in tune with his constant push to investigate anything and everything. Yet, her orderly nature kept him anchored.

One Saturday we planned to do some baking. The recipe called for margarine, which Grandma retrieved from the fridge. It was a new batch of white, tasteless stuff looking like lard and encased in a plastic bag. (A Minnesota regulation prohibited the sale of colored margarine –this stayed on the books for a long time after the end of World War II. It was said that dairy farmers pressured the legislature.) Butter wasn't readily available, so the homemaker had to color margarine herself: first you brought it to room temperature, then you squeezed open a small orange-colored capsule within the plastic wrap, and finally you kneaded the margarine until its color was distributed. Uniform golden color was an achievement, for streaks often appeared in the "butter" dish at the dinner table, reminding us of our sacrificing for the War.

On that Saturday, Grandma said, "I'm tired of this kneading – let's just play catch with this thing – the color will get worked into it." Margarine catch with Grandma! Back and forth we threw the package, laughing and encouraging each other. Then one of us fumbled, the plastic cylinder fell, broke open, and partly colored margarine splattered all over the linoleum. Everywhere. Streaky bits of yellow-y-white-ish fat splayed out in a radiating pattern. That was the end of margarine toss as an antidote to boredom. I know we cleaned up, but I'd like to think a large-enough pile permitted Grandma to salvage some off the top. Did she figure that oven heat would take care of germs?

Other routines, such as dinner dishes, could become playful. Grandma washed and rinsed while I dried, looking out the window over the sink, and into the vegetable garden. (When she had worked with contractors to build houses, she always made sure to place a window over the sink.)

We used a World War II device for soap bits: a box-shaped wire basket on a long handle, with a door that snapped shut. Into this basket we put leftover pieces of Ivory Soap. By swishing this in the water we produced suds from thrift. As we worked, we made up poems with absolute rhymes, and phrases with thumpy meters. I found one in my scrapbook written in my elementary school handwriting.

Day and Night

The sun is bright,
The air is soft,
And in the night
The moons aloft.

The flowers bloom,
The children play,
The birds in tune
Sing all the day.

And in the eve,
The sun goes down,
The shadows weave
Around the town.

(Signed) by Clara Dickey Parsons and Janet Parsons

Sometimes the poems became songs we sang together.

My adventures with Grandma weren't explorations of grand landscapes, although she had done that, too, on a trip to Europe when Dad was fifteen, and on another trip to see the Mayan ruins in 1948. Those journeys had involved dreaming, guidebook consultations, planning sessions, language brush-ups, and savings accounts. Adventures including me were of the moment.

One night in another summer, I had just settled into my top bunk bed when I looked through the window and saw flames. It looked like a bonfire of raked leaves and fallen twigs – but it was in the wrong place, at the wrong time of year. I could see it through tree trunks crowding the vacant lot beyond our yard. It must have been early summer, for the undergrowth wasn't blocking my view.

The fire wasn't *in* the vacant lot, but seemed to be on Grimes Avenue, one block over and parallel to our street.

I climbed down. Carol followed; Dudley was asleep. We tumbled downstairs to the living room where Grandma, Grandpa and Dad sat in their robes, reading and sipping their evening coffee.

"We can see a fire on Grimes Avenue!" The adults hurried to the bay window to peer past the backyard and through the vacant lot; flames now burned higher.

"Let's go see what it is!" This came from Grandma.

"But we're in our pajamas!"

"Oh, that doesn't matter. No one will care. It's warm out. Just get your bathrobes, and we'll go."

In our pajamas, bathrobes, and slippers, we went out the front door, walked past four houses to 42nd street, turned left down the short block, and then up Grimes Avenue. Grandpa stayed behind; Dad went to his room to read.

A car was burning. A wheel was outlined black against the flames. We moved closer, saw a few neighbors gathering and murmuring. We moved back from the heat but no one said, "Get away! There could be an explosion!" The village constable wasn't there. Perhaps he'd been busy; perhaps no one had called him. We watched for a while, and then it was time to go.

Grandma, Carol, and I went back around the block to return home, our bathrobes cover against the breeze, our slippers silent on the sidewalk. We never learned whose car that was, or why it had been abandoned, or what caused the fire. If our grandparents found out, then they didn't tell us. But I saw my proper Grandma escorting us down the street, feet pointed out, dressed in her nightclothes, ready for bed.

I wanted to become like her.

CHAPTER 9

Excursions with Grandpa

———

THE MENDOTA BRIDGE WAS THE worst. I can see Grandpa charging ahead with his stiff-legged limp. We were behind him – Dudley, Carol, and I – in single file, four of us crossing the bridge in the pedestrian lane. How did we get there? We must have taken street-cars and buses, rattling and transferring our way to Fort Snelling or Mendota Heights.

How do two retired people, in their sixties, find activities for three growing children? All the adults, Dad included, needed to find creative, free, or cheap ways to improve our leisure time. This challenge was Grandpa's opportunity! He could share his love of local history! He could involve us in his stories!

Excursions filled the bill.

I understand why he chose the Mendota Bridge. At the time, people considered it a marvel: the longest continuous concrete arch bridge in the world, not far from the confluence of the Minnesota and Mississippi Rivers. ("Mendota" means "meeting of the waters" in the Dakota language.) Maybe Grandma needed us out of the house, so she could renew her energy. And Grandpa would travel anywhere.

As he forged ahead on the walkway, he would have had us turn to face an early army outpost built to protect settlers: "There it is! Fort Snelling!" He might have talked about Turner and Wheeler, engineers who designed the concrete wonder. (Wheeler had spoken at the Saturday Lunch Club in 1931.) He would have described the construction of thirteen arches spanning the Minnesota River, nearly a mile long.

The crossing felt like five miles. Grandpa had chosen good weather for the excursion – no rain, snow, or fog. But also no Alden Drive elms to shade us. Just sun. Broiling, inescapable sun. The light breeze, found on any river, did nothing to cool us.

"How much longer?"

"Just a little bit." Said with cheer.

I don't remember hats. Only sweat dripping down my forehead, into my eyes, off the end of my nose. We trudged. That's what it was like: three of us in single file behind Grandpa, enduring heat, failing the enthusiasm test, looking at our feet instead of his arm swinging around to point out sights.

Was he aware of our misery, believing that the outing was more important? Believing that Parsons don't give up? Did we even pack a lunch?

Today, I might exclaim to my grandchildren about simultaneous views of Minneapolis and St. Paul, the River's flats and islands, canoes and vacation steamboats, airplanes taking off and landing at Lindbergh International Airport. It would be discovery time. We'd see these through windows of an air-conditioned car.

The Foshay Tower was better. We could reach it with one streetcar ride and a short walk. Grandpa took me there for a panoramic view of Minneapolis and beyond. At the time, it was the tallest building in the city, built to imitate the Washington Monument. Perhaps Carol and Dudley came along; maybe they had separate tours.

We entered the Art Deco lobby, found the elevator, and rode to the top floor. Grandpa stood me in front of the windows and pointed out the Mississippi River, Lake Calhoun, Lake Harriet, and Lake of the Isles. He told his story of the Pond Brothers, who were missionaries to a Dakota tribe while in their summer camp at the edge of Lake Harriet. He showed me Hennepin Avenue and how its elbow bend changed the direction.

Today the Foshay Tower's Art Deco lobby is restored. A small museum and observation deck are on the 31st floor. Some taller buildings stand next to it, but as far as I can tell, one can still see Hennepin Avenue from the deck.

I was older for the art exhibit. Grandpa took me to view the "Berlin Masterpieces." This was a group of paintings hidden by the Nazis during World War II. The US Army had later discovered and shipped them to the National Gallery of Art in Washington, D.C. for safekeeping. Before returning them to Germany, a selection of these canvasses became a traveling exhibit, with a stay at the Minneapolis Institute of Art in 1948. Newspapers in the Twin Cities gave strong publicity to the "Berlin Masterpieces," so it was a given that Parsons would make their way to the museum.

After climbing steps to the main entrance, we paid our admission and found the specified galleries. It was crowded. Adults craned necks and moved heads to glimpse paintings through small openings between viewers' shoulders. Sometimes people nudged others aside and pushed forward. That was Grandpa's style. We rounded a corner, elbowed to the front of the crowd, and stood next to a protective rope. His voice boomed out: "Oh! She's *big!* And *naked!*"

The painting was of a woman whose enormous breasts drooped onto her midriff. I don't think a cloth covered her thighs and lower belly. She seemed to overflow the entire canvas, although I recall seeing angelic attendants peeking through greenery. Perhaps this was a Titian.

I was thirteen and needed to disappear. Other viewers seemed not to notice Grandpa's voice trumpeting over the room, but I knew they were laughing at me. I was certain they'd tell their neighbors, friends, and relatives about us, as soon as they could get home and pick up the phone.

Despite my embarrassment, this excursion took. When an adult, I began to visit art museums, and discovered quiet renewal in contemplating a painting. Museum trips became a favorite way to be with friends as we pointed out to each other graceful lines on ancient Iranian pottery, details in Moghul miniatures, or the delicate carvings on the netsukes used to fasten Japanese kimono cords.

When my son Eric was young, I took him to the Museum of Fine Arts in Boston every Saturday morning for several years. During his two-hour art lesson, I wandered the galleries. I discerned personality in Copley's portraits, and re-visited early American furniture. I laughed out loud at Calder's miniature circus, with its mechanical figurines scooping up tiny elephant droppings. After an hour, I sat under skylights sipping coffee in the first floor café, watching visitors. Then it was time to meet Eric and return home to Saturday laundry.

As Eric became older, my second son Steven took his place. They both developed an interest in making art, but Eric did especially. Today he supports his family with skills in graphics, and continues to paint. Steven finds relaxation from his work through drawing and sculpting.

Visiting art museums is still one of my favorite outings but I don't know if it will take root in my grandchildren. I recall a summer years after those museum excursions: I'm running my Granny Nanny Camp for Steven's children Dylan and Jessica, about ten and eight years old. I need to get out of the house, leave the neighborhood, and improve their minds. We visit the Museum of the American Indian.

"Here we are! Let's see the movie first!" As the movie plays, I *think* they're following it. On to the next floor: "Look at all this beautiful beadwork!" I'm pointing to an open drawer displaying a vest covered in intricate design. There's a video on the wall above, which shows the same beadwork that's right in front of them. They're watching the video and ignoring the real thing.

In thirty minutes they're finished. "Let's check out the Dakota exhibit! They lived where I grew up!"

"No." They lean against a railing and cross their arms.

How did I fail to foresee that their high point is lunch and the gift shop? Or *is* there a spark of interest, hidden from me? Is their experience *that* different from mine? And why, a week later, don't they respond to my hook: "Let's go to the National Gallery! We'll have a contest about who can find the most pictures of naked ladies."

"I don't want to."

"Nah."

My grandparents had less money than I, but were more inventive in ways to use time, to arouse curiosity, to try to teach something. Because of their tight budget, excursions were their mode of choice. They didn't have a TV or video games to entice. Even though my grandchildren will put my ideas in second, third, or fourth place when measured against TV, basketball courts, and neighborhood friends, I still try to lure them into cultural forays – with one hundred percent hope, and unknown chances for success.

CHAPTER 10

"Travel-itus"

———

MY GRANDPARENTS LOVED TRAVEL. THEY often told about their 1921 journey to Spain, France and England. This was the "To Europe on a Cow" trip, when they had paid for their travels by saving all the money earned through selling milk to the neighbors. Dad was fourteen, Uncle Edgar ten. They left four-year-old Ernest at home with relatives because he was thought too young and fragile to join them. He had a "weak heart," explained Grandma.

The 1921 trip had occurred when the post World War I dollar gained in value against inflated European currencies. That's when they made their first airplane flight. Years later when I was middle-aged, Dad and I were having breakfast as he tossed that story to me: "We were in Paris when my mother came up with the idea of flying across the Channel. She made the arrangements. The pilot drove all the way into Paris, picked us up at the hotel, and drove us back to Le Bourget Airport. We turned out to be the only passengers. It was one of those bi-planes, and we sat in wicker seats bolted to the floor."

"Did the pilot wear a leather hat and jacket, like those pictures of men standing next to their planes?" I could see scarves fluttering.

His "ye-e-e-es" meant that Dad wasn't sure, but wanted to please me, and liked the embellishment.

"To Europe on a Cow" ensured Grandpa's transmitting his "travel-itus gene" to Dad. Dad had been twenty-two when he applied to teach at Woodstock School in India. After two years of persistence, he received his appointment as a science teacher and sailed in June 1930, to stay for six and one-half years. After three years of correspondence – they had met as schoolteachers in Aitken, Minnesota – my mother joined him in 1933. They married immediately and I was born eighteen months later.

They filled their letters from India with wonders of discovering a different culture, gaining ability in Hindi, and initiating creative school programs. They described travels to Agra, Jaipur, and Ajmer, expressed amazement at temples and forts, and repeated their longing to see family members. "How I wish I could have a cup of coffee with you," my mother wrote to her father, sister, and in-laws.

It was inevitable that they'd invite my grandparents to visit. Dad initiated the dialogue in 1934, and Grandpa needed no prodding. He planned, reviewed plans, revised plans and shifted plans. These travel dreams were recreation: "I have just been having another orgy of travel-itus inspired by the arrival from the Republic of Lebanon, otherwise Syria, of information about accommodations over the desert from Bayroute[sic] to Bagdad . . ." [14]

Grandpa wanted to travel to India by an exotic route – a straight boat ride from New York to Bombay wouldn't do. 1936, all agreed, would be the best time for the family, including Ernest, to arrive in India. They would return to the States with my parents and me. For more than a year, Grandpa investigated prices, changed routes, and altered dates. He even considered risking the early onset of the unpleasant monsoons.

That plan morphed into a return via the Khyber Pass and Afghanistan:

Speaking of the Khyber – that's where we want to go after seeing you in 1936, and through the pass to Kabul, the capital
of Afghanistan. No steaming plains for us in the month of
July, even if we have to miss the burning ghats and the wonders of Benares. We can't hope to see everything, anyhow....
Before we leave, we shall write the Emir of Afghanistan so that
he will receive us. My reading for the last forty years has filled
my head with pictures of processions of invaders from 1500
B.C. down to 1620 A.D., flowing through the Khyber Pass and
I want to stand on the ground that Ghenghis, Tamerlane and
Bahir traversed.[15]

The Emir of Afghanistan? What was he thinking? I suppose he hoped
to interview the ruler.

Yet, his ideas weren't entirely off the map, for he added to his
pension with honoraria from speaking engagements, and that possibility was always in mind:

India! We all are dreaming, dreaming of that journey.
Different maps and ocean routes appeal to us. Just now I am
amusing myself with projecting a trip through Russia to a
point in Asia where the Turkestan Railroad runs southward
to Bokhara, and wondering how we'd get from Bokhara
through the Himalayas to your house. Probably we can't do
it. Or, can we travel by caravan from a point on the Black
Sea.... Now, tell me what the caravan fare will be? The entire journey around the world is $450. But this world jour-
ney is, after all, conventional whereas a trip across Persia
might contain elements enough of uniqueness to justify a
lyceum bureau dating us up for a few talks. We feel that we
are good enough to buy. Your mother is making an enviable
reputation as a public speaker and should go over strong

presenting to women's clubs and other groups the domestic angle of various racial problems while I discuss the economic and political phases. She is modest but I believe I can sell her the idea.[16]

Grandpa interpreted her response as "modesty," but it might have been simple resistance. She knew his gigantic enthusiasms didn't always work out, and she likely considered it best to take a wait-and-see approach.

Ernest got involved in trying to put on the brakes:

Dad has set himself to the job of completely exhausting the possible routes and lines and etc., which will take us to India, with an eye out for the cheapest company or route which will give us the most comfortable voyage during which we may be most interested. He is, just now, canvassing the possibility of crossing the Soviet Union. He has the price whittled down to where it begins to look remotely as if we might make it and before we know it, they will be paying us money to go! . . . I have assumed the role of the skeptic for the purpose of keeping the family's feet on the ground while we work the thing out on a sane basis.[17]

Grandpa planned to finance this trip with sales of his book, *The Government of Minnesota*, to the public schools. It had done well: its first printing was sold out, and a second one ordered. He hoped to earn enough, in spite of the Depression and tight school budgets, to finance their trip. He kept rearranging the household income and expense columns. He kept on dreaming. Ideas continued to shift shape from traveling through Russia to staying in a village on the Don River for ten weeks. Finally, Dad wrote a clear response to Grandpa's plans for traveling through Central Asia:

I have been following Dad's plans to come to India by this and that "unconventional route" with a great deal of interest...but however much I understand it, I cannot bring myself to support his routes. There are two important reasons for this. (1.) <u>I believe that you do want to come to India...</u>. Therefore, I think that you should plan to make it <u>the focus of your plans</u> – the route to, and the route from, should be subsidiary. (2.) I suppose that it will be impossible to convince you of this, but the Central Asia routes that Dad proposes following are definitely dangerous. The inhabitants are far from being the kindly, hospitable, sympathetic people that we found everywhere in Spain, for instance, or in Morningside; instead, they are grasping, unscrupulous, all ready to take advantage of the inexperienced and unwary traveler. And that you are inexperienced, at least with respect to travel in Oriental countries, I think neither of you can seriously doubt.

Thus, the advice Luella and I have to give you is this: take the most direct route from America to India that you can manage...stay in India as long as you can, and go directly home.[18]

References to that journey soon disappear from the letters. The India plans never appear again. A year later, Grandpa mentioned an idea for a trip to Europe and a visit to relatives in Wiltshire, England with Ernest. There's a gap in the collection of letters, so I'll never know what happened. I suppose money couldn't be found.

Circumstances prevented my grandparents' visiting other places they longed to see: a Depression Era budget, then World War II, our move into their home, and health problems. However, they had made some trips within the United States all along, and always by bus. They saw Williamsburg, Virginia

(Grandpa wrote in "Parsonalities," "In experiencing these joys we have almost forgiven Rockefeller for his capitalistic exploitations."[19] Other travels included Gettysburg, Pennsylvania, and the Chicago World's Fair. Grandpa had gone to Winnipeg to see the renowned Dionne Quintuplets christen a battleship. He had seen the King and Queen of England during their wartime visit to Canada. (He used *Hennepin County Review* press passes to push in close to the action.)

But as they became tethered to Alden Drive, Grandpa read his *Encyclopedia Britannica* atlas and wrote in its endpapers and flyleaves, where he jotted his acceptance of their limits: "The spot in which we are called to live is one we come to love. But we shouldn't be confined by it. Rather we should in spirit range the world. December 15, 1946" [20]

In 1948, my grandparents undertook a three months' journey to the Yucatan Peninsula. Grandma's health had begun to fail but she insisted on her dream. I know they enjoyed planning and saving for this trip, which took place after we moved from their home, to 4437 Brookside Terrace. Once I saw Grandma descending the short flight of stairs from their bedroom over the garage, wearing her amber beads. She must have been on her way to her bridge club, PEO meeting, church group, or speaking engagement. With energy in her step, she held up a book, talked about Mexican history and culture, told me about practicing her Spanish, and spoke a few words to demonstrate.

They took buses all the way: first to Ohio, to welcome my newborn cousin Polly, who had been born that January. New Orleans was next, visiting "Negro Colleges at Talladega and Tuskegee" on the way. After some time in the Yucatan peninsula based in Merida, they visited Mexico City for a week before returning home. As soon as they could share stories, their enthusiasm for this adventure spilled all over us.

The "travel-itus gene" has emerged in each generation. Dad and my stepmother Margaret went to Norway three times to visit relatives. Dad learned Norwegian to make this easier, and Margaret brushed up on hers. I've traveled in North America, Western Europe, and India, but principally in France and Russia. (Instead of wanting to try every new route as Grandpa had dreamed, I like to return to places I've learned to love. Or so I say.) Both Eric and Steven have been on some of these trips, and Steven carries on, having lived and worked in Russia. My grandchildren Dylan and Jessica have been back and forth to Russia. The traveling part of the story isn't finished.

CHAPTER 11
Ernest's Shadow

———

A BLURRY FIGURE – A DARK shadow – skis off the photo's edge. It's the leafless trees in the orchard that are in focus and centered. How do I know the blur is Uncle Ernest? His face isn't there; there's no way to tell. Now I remember: I've seen this album before. This time, I lift the photo to find a note: "Me skiing." Uncle Ernest must have started this album about himself. But he didn't finish it.

"He had heart problems," Grandma said one day at dinner-time when Ernest's ghost was raised – the day I first heard his name, when I was about ten. Maybe he was mentioned in connection with the happy story of "Going to Europe on a Cow," which Grandpa referred to several times in his *Hennepin County Review* column:

Thirty Years in Morningside
There was a cow – or rather, there were several through the years – that, besides giving us all the milk that we could use, made us a purse of $2,100.00. On the sum, all but the youngest of us went to France, Spain and England for the summer – an unforget-table summer![21]

Grandma, too, wrote about that trip in a lively story titled "En Marcha!" She detailed the family's dreams for the journey: "Dad" wanted to go to England, "Big Brother" (my father) wanted to see

Spain, and "Little Brother" (Uncle Edgar) wanted to explore an American city en route. She described how they narrowed their choices to Chicago, Spain, France, and England. She named frustrations with obtaining passports and visas. She showed us suitcases being packed. We learned about the kitchen utensil kit and that an iron, turned upside down, became a hotplate to boil water. She invited us to walk streets in Spanish cities with her.

But she didn't refer to Ernest.

My grandparents had left him at home; they thought he was too young and frail, at four years old, to join the family. Who took care of him? It must have been relatives. Did my grandparents think he would forget being left behind?

Maybe his ghost was raised when Grandpa talked about Upton Sinclair, who had come to dinner and spent the evening. "He took Ernest and set him on his knee. He spoke to Ernest in such a gentle way – after that, Ernest's stutter went away." Grandma gave a look, which told me the healing was temporary.

Maybe he was mentioned that dinnertime in connection with Grandpa's book *Heroes of the Northwest*, biographical sketches written for ten-year-olds. Ernest, twelve or thirteen years old, had provided illustrations. There's one on the maroon cover: a road with cart and horse, followed by an open car. His drawings are sprinkled throughout the book: Sitting Bull is killed, William Mayo arrives in town, and John Lind assaults a man. It was clever and affirming for Grandpa to choose Ernest as his illustrator.

On that day, conversation faded after Grandma's reference to heart problems. I concluded he'd died of heart disease. Forever after, whenever Ernest was named, his loss was palpable. His shadow hovered: there was an edging away from the subject of Ernest, a fidgeting, a change of topic. An avoidance of pain.

"He had heart problems." It was true. He did have heart problems, but he didn't die of heart disease, literally. He died on August 1, 1937, when he was nineteen years old. Uncle Edgar told me about it the year I lived with my aunt and uncle in Maryland. I was twenty-one; it was eleven years after I first heard Ernest's name. "He came home one night after going out with a girl. She'd rebuffed him. He went upstairs to his room and shot himself."

Someone – my grandparents? The police? Another family member? Someone found a diary with entries seeming to indicate that Ernest had planned suicide. When Edgar added that detail, he wasn't looking at me; he was seeing something overwhelming. He had been twenty-five, and was the one to identify his little brother before the cremation – that was the law, he told me. "I'll never forget having to see that body before it went into the furnace. It was horrible. Your Dad couldn't come – he was in India." Edgar began to cry. I took his account into my heart to ponder.

But my father was not in India when Ernest died, because we had returned four months beforehand, in March 1937, when I was two. I suppose Dad couldn't face the responsibility of identifying Ernest, and it fell to Uncle Edgar to stand there in the crematorium. When Edgar told his story, it didn't occur to me to write Dad for more information. Maybe I wanted to protect him. Now I have an idea about his pain.

When I dip into my family's letters back and forth from Morningside to India I come across references to Ernest and his friends. They mention his graduation from West High School in Minneapolis, his jobs as a newspaper carrier, and his plans to enter an art program at the University of Minnesota. I remember one in which Grandma thanked Dad for giving Ernest Dad's own '22'. He couldn't take it to India, so left it for his young brother to use. I'll always wonder if this was the gun that Ernest used on himself. What a horrible burden for Dad. Guns weren't unusual in their culture then. No one in my family uses one now, although my brother Dudley once bought a rifle – I think he was in college at the time. He did this against Dad's protests. Dudley couldn't comprehend Dad's vehemence.

My understanding expanded when I found a paragraph from "The Morningsider" among Grandpa's newspaper columns.

Ernest Parsons

"In short measures life may perfect be." So said the English poet Ben Johnson, and...it did not occur to me that I should ever want to mark the passing of my own son with these words, treasures though they be; but after the sharp sorrow of his death this day, how can I escape the truth that they convey....

We shall be truer to trust, hardier to endure, and stronger in the charity "that suffereth long and is kind" because we have known him. Every day we shall know of his approval of the things we do sincerely. Son, your place will never be vacant.[22]

Was this all? It was hard to accept. It seemed like a minimal reaction to a son's death. Now I realize it wasn't minimal. Grandpa wrote this immediately after Ernest's death, facing it in his own way. He wouldn't have thought it appropriate to splash feelings all over the paper. Still, I was relieved to find his verses later on in another "Morningsider:"

To Ernest Parsons
October 16, 1917 – August 1, 1937

Son, would you not await the blossoming
Of your bright future? Could you not abide
The passing of the storm and, like the robins, sing
Away the clouds that your serenity denied?...

Why did I leave you lonely, stricken down
By bitter questions, drenched by fear,

Tempestuous, while some unfeeling clown
Made instant claim upon my idle ear?...

And through the years remaining yet to me,
I'll listen to your soul sing boldly out
From records of your living symphony,
And in your spirit answer every doubt.[23]

Now we know that people didn't talk about these things at the
time – there were no support groups, no therapists, no family
conferences. Perhaps there was a decision to shield us while we
were young, for our mother's loss was still fresh when we lived
with Grandma and Grandpa. Why name Ernest's death a suicide
to children six, eight and ten? For the sake of protecting us, they
protected themselves.

That no-talk rule can be found in my grandfather's little pamphlet *Clara Dickey Parsons*, a short biography – a praise-song – written
about my grandmother after she died in 1951. It holds one reference
to Ernest's death:

> Our youngest son – Ernest – who had had a weak heart from
> childhood, died in August 1937, and Clara never recovered
> from the blow. She so blamed herself for not doing her duty
> by him that I was forced to tell her not to speak to me about
> it again. For, said I, "The past cannot be redeemed. You
> did your full duty. It will only make you ill to dwell in re-
> morseful sorrow upon your actions that only you think were
> inadequate."[24]

Every so often I was invited further back into the event. As Dad
and I sat at the kitchen table one day in the nineteen-nineties,
Dad mentioned Ernest, and said, referring to his mother, "She was
never the same." Who would be? The brief obituary, of which I

have only a copy, does not include the kind and gentle formula "he died suddenly."

E. Dudley Parsons'
Son, Ernest, 19, Dies

Ernest Parsons, 19, son of Mr. and Mrs. E. Dudley Parsons of 4210 Alden Drive, Morningside, died early Sunday in Northwestern hospital. He had been taken there only a few hours before, after he had been found in his bedroom by his mother. There was a bullet wound in his head, and by his side was a small caliber rifle.[25]

"She was never the same." And my father wasn't, either. "My father wanted me to talk to him," Dad continued. I had the impression that he had indeed "talked to" Ernest but it didn't work. But about what? What was the subject of this "talk?" I didn't ask. Now I wonder if Dad might have been open to questions. It wasn't our family practice to probe, or even pursue leads when painful subjects arose.

Another time, someone asked Dad about his name: "Does the "E." stand for Ernest, like your Father's name?" "No, it's just the initial. I took it for my own after Ernest died." Grandpa was Ernest Dudley, Dad became E. Dudley, my brother is Ernest Dudley. It's as though we had to carry him with us. His name *had* to go on. *He* had to go on.

My understanding continued to stretch. When 4437 Brookside Terrace was sold in 2005, I received the photo album that I now turn to again. Ernest is in a tracksuit (his heart trouble didn't prevent his being on a track team); he's dancing with someone named Irene under a plum tree; he's with her on a tire swing. He's seated pensively in the orchard; he's on a sled fixed up with a sail; he's coming off a ship called the SS Huronic. He labeled this one "entering America." In all these pictures, his body looks soft.

And then I see him dressed in women's clothes.

An unattributed clipping is pasted next to the picture:

Man to Take Feminine Lead

A young man will take the feminine lead in *Path Across the Hill,* a play to be held at the Morningside Community Church . . . [26]

Grandpa wrote to Dad about Ernest's success:

Last night he performed magnificently as a girl in a play. You should have seen his entrance in a red dress, blond wig, and a dashing manner! The audience was tickled to death. Some didn't even recognize that he was a boy until after the performance. He says that next time he must have "a manly part" however; and I believe he will do that as well![27]

Five months later, another letter from Grandpa to Dad said that Ernest had been asked to play a woman a second time: "Ernest came in with a problem as to whether or not he should take a girl's part again in the Christian Endeavor play. We discussed this problem in all its aspects until mother rolled over asleep and Ernest began to prepare for bed." [28]

If Ernest was reluctant, then he must have been persuaded: "Ernest is on the last lap of his practice as Peggy in a play to be given at the church hall (the best south of Lake Street) on December 10th. We all expect to enjoy him and the other kids in their performance."[29]

Ernest might have been gay, or bisexual, or trans-gendered, or a cross-dresser. He might have wondered "who am I, in my heart? Am I attracted to men? Women? Both?" I know it's possible that his suicide was a response to an unfulfilled "boy-girl" romance. I could be wrong about his sexuality. But a struggle with sexuality feels right, fits with my memories of family tone whenever his name came up.

When Dad was commissioned to "talk to" Ernest, it might have been to persuade him to be more interested in women. I'm not sure about this "talk." It's my conclusion. It's in keeping with the belief, more prevalent then, that sexuality is a rational decision. I look at his pictures, and think: *everyone must have struggled with questions about Ernest's sexual orientation, with dim or clear comprehension, within themselves or in surface conversation, in silence or by slanted words.* I'll never know for sure, but Grandma's statement "he had heart problems" was both emotionally and physically true. My family's response to his death was in keeping with their times, and it had its consequences.

Psychologists who consider family systems have said that a family works to replace its loss – often without realizing it. *Yes. Dad took his initial; my brother has his name. Is that why Grandpa and then Dad kept his sketchbooks and passed them down?* I have one of these sketchbooks, full of exercises, swiftly executed with a sure hand. A few are finished drawings. I framed one. It's a political cartoon showing two stout men wearing fur coats, smoking cigars, and watching a group of marchers who carry banners proclaiming, "On Strike!" One man is unshaven, another is badly dressed, and a woman is among them. All look subdued and determined. One of the watching men comments: "That's the trouble with these Reds... give 'em a little and they always want more." Ernest had absorbed his parents' concerns about justice. When I saw the sketches: *Yes. That* was *a loss, and not only for the family.*

He had a fine talent. And so does my elder son, Eric, a figurative painter and graphic designer. Eric seemed to have been born with his talent, but from the start I nurtured it with a fierceness I didn't comprehend. I provided art supplies, drove him to art lessons, applauded his canvasses, visited him in art school, and saw his exhibits. My father received his pictures happily, and inquired about his progress. When Dad handed me, to give to Eric, a portfolio of Ernest's drawings and sketches, I received the message *These must be kept safe and handed on.* An affirmation of Eric's talent. Maybe a burden. Through the years, I held to myself an unnamed fear that didn't come to pass: *artists commit suicide.* I didn't discuss Ernest's death with Eric until he was a young man. I, too, was trying to replace the family's loss.

And now I return to the album to look at its close, which Grandma must have completed. There's a commercial Rustcraft card – a little puppy with a shiny glass tear coming from his eye. The caption reads "Aint you never coming back?" Finally, there are two pictures of Ernest: his high school graduation picture and one in which he's dressed in a pinstriped suit, hat, white shirt and tie. A manly outfit. The album closes with Ernest's drawing of Grandma – she's darning a sock. Underneath, she has written "Su Madre."

"He had heart problems." The whole family has heart pain, under his shadow, as he forever disappears off the edge of the picture.

CHAPTER 12

The Garden

———

BOOKS, NEWSPAPERS, AND SATURDAY LUNCH Club programs fueled
Grandpa's contributions to Sunday dinner times. Dad also enjoyed
good debate; his thinking style was linear, so he armed himself
with facts, figures, and logic to challenge his father. Sometimes,
however, Grandma's compressed lips slowed the talk. She shared
Grandpa's views, but preferred subtle expressions, clever questions, and fewer stubborn declarations. Grandma's responses sent
the subject veering, for a time, toward topics such as how to improve the minister's sermon, or whether tomatoes were ripening
as expected.

Their garden wasn't a small matter during table talk. I see
this garden today, over sixty years later, as I mentally place
myself again on my perch in the elm tree, book in hand. I'm
not reading. Rather, I'm impressed with the *idea* of reading
while sitting on the hard knobby vee formed by two branches.
Impressed, too, by my having shinnied up while wearing shorts.
My legs smart and sting from the climb, but I'm pleased with my
ten-year-old self.

From this seat, I peer through graceful elm branches at parts
of the back yard, nearly half an acre in all. Next to the house,
flowers bloom. There, too, sits the small pool enclosed by a rock
wall, filled with water lilies, and replenished with the hose each
day. As I turn my head, the lacy willow tree obstructs my view of

the orchard, but not of the long, full vegetable garden. This is the garden that feeds both our bodies and our souls at dinnertime, although I'm not awake to that deeper meaning while high in the elm.

Today, I recall how Grandpa had demonstrated his love for creation at that same tree. He was taking me on a tour of the back yard. "Do you know your trees? This is an elm tree. Look at the smooth bark. Now stand back and look at its shape – like a tall vase with branches drooping all around. We must take care of our trees." He pulled me over to the small orchard – at least one plum, a cherry, and several apple trees descending on the southern slope, planted so each would catch the sun.

"Look! Here's my new graft." He took out his pocketknife and sliced into the warm air, as he described his accomplishment. He had removed the end of a small branch, made a lengthwise incision in the stump, inserted a leafy twig into the opening, wrapped the area with moistened cloth, clamped it all together with stripped twigs on either side, and bound the whole with cord. "I'm hoping that the graft will take – then we'll have a new kind of apple growing on this tree!"

With a short walk from the orchard we could reach the vegetable garden. Grandpa had planted rows of sweet corn, peas, beans, lettuce, tomatoes, carrots and potatoes. He often described gardening in "The Morningsider:"

Gardening in June

"Then, if ever come the perfect days," so said Lowell, as every schoolboy knows. But Lowell was not a gardener and consequently didn't know half of the sweet story of the planting, the cultivating and the harvesting of garden crops. Generally, by the 15th of June we serve peas fresh from the row. Let no one think that the best pea in the stalls can compare with that that is picked, shelled and cooked within an hour. Flavor departs from all garden stuff from the moment it leaves the soil, but the pea is the first to lose it. The young onions from the sets that were planted as soon as the ground had thawed out are a joy to the breakfaster. My friends, do not care that someone will detect the odor of onions on your breath; but avail yourself of the God-given chance to eat the succulent stalks with bread and butter. Asparagus grows freely wherever afforded a lodgment for the birds carry the seeds from place to place. And how delightful to break off the tender shoots rather than contemplate chewing the twig-like restaurant offering! The rhubarb (I like to call it by the good American name, "pie-plant") is a never failing source of pleasure, for a very few roots will not only serve the family but friends as well. Our beans are flowering and will call to us soon to take them to the pot. They are prolific; a short row will feed a family all the summer long and the winter as well.

A friend who fancies bulldogs told me the other day that he had found that gardens do not pay since the green grocers provide so efficiently for all vegetable needs – but I felt that I had him at last on even terms when I replied: "Neither do bulldogs pay."[30]

Because Grandpa was an organic gardener – except for his fruit trees, which he sprayed – he once gave each of us children a small can filled with kerosene. Potato bugs were appearing and feeding on the potato plants. One afternoon he ordered us (this was framed as a wonderful new project) to hand pick bugs off the leaves and drop them into the can. We finished one row.

Since we were of little practical help in Grandpa's garden, his purpose must have been instruction. Some of his teaching landed in me: when I had my own garden at last, it felt "right" to turn compost and hand-pull dandelions with an old table knife.

"Here's a bushel basket." Grandpa seemed energized as he handed it over to us three children on a Saturday afternoon. He held several old table knives in his hand. "When this basket is full, I'll buy ice cream for all of us!" (A bushel is 37 quarts!) He returned to his hoe. We began to dig the deep-rooted weeds out of the lawn, sprinkling clover seed into the remaining holes. It didn't take long to realize that this basket could never be filled by suppertime.

Grandma arrived and made her assessment. She returned with old newspapers. "I have an idea. Let's crumple up these newspapers and put them in the bottom of the basket. Then we'll spread dandelions on top and get our ice cream." Within an hour our entire bushel basket was "filled," and we called Grandpa over to see our work. He knew what had gone on, I'm sure. The vanilla ice cream was delicious.

Today, growing vegetables at home seems optional, especially in prosperous times, and in some neighborhoods. But my grandparents, their friends, and neighbors all assumed that gardens were essential. It was the topic of conversation whenever Grandpa met someone on the sidewalk, and of course he could turn gardening into a political matter.

A case had been made before the village council. If Grandpa wasn't the presenter, then he rallied the neighbors; if he didn't lead the rally, then he wrote letters to support the cause. But he was involved, given his sparkle as he burst through the door one day, to announce, "The village will allow gardens in the unused land across the street." It wasn't long before those Victory Gardens, and our own, appeared in "Parsonalities:"

Fun with The Seed Catalog
It is time to make out the seed list for the Victory Garden of 1945. Yes, this new lettuce, No. 169. Look it up in the index.

Where is the index? In the front. No, in the back. It isn't indexed. Must be. No. It isn't. Well, put down Mammoth lettuce. They won't have more than one Mammoth. And, say, let's have spinach this year....Peas! We've got to raise twice as many as last year. No lima beans – I don't like 'em. Oh, do you? Well, one row then. No use trying melons with all those kids about. But we must have more potatoes. Yes, Warbas. Hard to peel? Then a smoother kind. Here, these look good – in the picture – Majestic – "eight hills yields a peck." To get six bushels we need at least 192 hills. That Nankin cherry lost his bride last summer. We must marry him again. We need another apple tree and some berries and more strawberry plants. Ah, there we are -- $12.25 worth of ammunition that will help defeat the enemy.[31]

Grandpa crossed the street to see the Victory Gardens and discuss cultivation, planting, and harvesting. He dispensed opinions, gave advice, and assessed the quality of his neighbors' work. These gardens flourished in humus-rich land, shielded from the street by a thicket of trees and vines. "Wild cucumbers" grew at the edge of the tangle – at least, that's what we neighborhood kids called the vine's fruit with its prickly knobs. We used these as weapons, slinging them in perpetual battle to defeat the invisible German army.

Gardening at home was mostly divided along gender lines: Grandpa managed the vegetables, orchard, and grass, while Grandma tended the flowers along the side of the house.

Neighbor Parsons Goes to Work in His Garden

And what, pray, is the little woman doing while I am moving, like a parish priest, among my garden folk? She is readying her flower beds for the bloom that surrounds us summer-long, due to her tireless care. By that neighborly trading that is characteristic of our community she has been able to enrich the yards of not a few of her friends. She holds, however, that flowers can be overdone just as the furniture of a house may be, that there is a certain sufficiency beyond which it is not good taste to go. Therefore she withholds her hand from tearing up too much of our sod and concentrates on two or three spots that yield to her efforts with surprising zeal, although now she is planning "just one new bed."[32]

In the back, delphiniums brightened the house's foundation. I can see their intense purple-y blue standing tall near the Lombardy Poplars. (Grandma had to have these poplars after seeing them in France.) The Minnesota artist Syd Fossum preserved these delphiniums and poplars in a watercolor. It's framed in apple wood from one of their fruit trees, and graces my living room wall, where I see it every day.

Grandpa's exuberant gardening began early in the morning. But Grandma had to rein him in (as in other areas of their life together):

Rules for Early Morning Work
The 'little woman' has laid down certain rules for my conduct in the yard and garden during the pre-breakfast period while she is taking the last fleeting cat-naps before coffee time. I give them to you for what they are worth:

1. Let the handles of rakes, broom or spade fall on sod, not on the sidewalk or other hard surface.
2. Use the fibre lawn broom only on the grass, not on a surface that produces a scratching sound.
3. Avoid the use of hedge shears.

4. Do not trundle a wheel barrow upon a hard surface and be sure it is well-oiled even if it travels on the grass.
5. No lawn cutting is permitted.
6. The whispering sickle is out, even if you can find it.
7. No hammering or sawing.
8. Remember everything you need in the course of your work so as to avoid entering the house until called and perhaps even going upstairs.
9. Do not talk to the paper carrier or the milk-man except by signs.
10. Think softly as you move about.

The penalty for breaking any one of these rules is the suspension of short-cake for the duration, and a second offense will mean the end of home-made bread.[33]

They joined together when preserving food to be shared, just as both preserved and shared family stories. Grandma canned beans and tomatoes; she turned cucumbers into pickles; she made apple jelly and strawberry jam. Together they harvested carrots, potatoes, and apples, then buried this produce in bushels of torn paper or sawdust for storage in the root cellar. We ate sweet corn or tomatoes as soon as they ripened: platters of sliced tomatoes, and heaped corn on the cob, soon to be slathered in butter. I loved those dinners. Some meals were comprised entirely of this captured sunshine and rich soil. "That's *all* you ate? That's *all*?" asked a friend years later as I described these suppers to her. Her shocked face told me she thought of them as meals of poverty, not of the plenty we knew.

I still think of those three years living with my grandparents as a bountiful time: a harvest of food, ideas, and discussion forming my feelings and attitudes. I received from them a reverence for the sacred dimension of mealtime. I heard lively discussion and respectful dialogue, and came to value this quality. They gave me the belief that travel can expand one's understanding of others – if it's treated as pilgrimage, I add now. They shared with us a commitment to equal access to resources (the "common wealth") as the context for individual freedom. And I feel connected with them when gardening.

4437 Brookside Terrace, Edina, Minnesota

CHAPTER 13
A Climate Change

———

DAD CAME HOME FROM WORK one day and invited me for a ride in the maroon Studebaker. He had recently gained a new job as Audio-Visual Consultant for the Minneapolis Public Schools, so we could afford a car. It was a sleek model with no running boards, a nose pointed out, and a recessing grill – a look that said "We're going forward!"

I got into the front seat with its plush upholstery, Dad shifted into first gear and we moved uphill toward Morningside Road. We had no destination – it was "just a ride." A misty atmosphere surrounded the car. The air hovered between fog and rain. I watched the windshield wipers swishing back and forth, back and forth, above the brown instrument panel. Something was up. Dad cleared his throat. Then he said, "Margaret and I have decided to get married." My stomach lurched. I stared out the windshield. *I'll stay with Grandma.*

Dad's voice lightened as he went on to describe the house they were purchasing: space for a picnic table, a hill in front for toboggans and sleds, the creek running below the hill for canoes and ice-skates. The plan was to move there soon.

My wordless unhappiness couldn't have been a surprise. When my mother knew she would die soon, she had worried about my response in a letter to a friend: " Of course I want Dudley to re-marry as soon as possible. . . . The children are so different. Janet will be 9 in December . . . she looks like me – and she is stubborn as are all of us in this family — I'm awfully afraid she will resent a stepmother . . . ." [34]

Since I was twelve and the eldest, Dad might have assumed that Mother's death impacted me more than it affected my siblings. No wonder he launched into a description of the new house, its attractions, and activities I might enjoy. I don't know if he had more to say about wedding plans.

I had always known Margaret. She was just over five feet tall, sturdy and plump. She wore her dark hair pinned around a roll called a "rat," which added body to her upsweep. My mother and hers were first cousins, so she shared the same Norwegian Great-Grandfather with Dudley, Carol, and me. This makes for a strange family tree. My stepmother and I are in the same generation — she was fifteen years older than I, and seventeen years younger than my mother. My half-brothers and I are also in the same generation, but only on my father's side. On Margaret's side, they occupy a spot in the next generation.

Margaret and her sister had come to holiday dinners, when wartime hospital work prevented their going home to the family farm a hundred miles west. During those meals, I always tried to sit next to her sister, who smiled. Margaret had taken care of us when Dudley was born nine years before. In an image so vivid I call it a "freeze-frame," I'm sitting on the living room rug, playing. Margaret is standing in the background. My mother has her coat on, her large belly pushing out, her bag in hand. She's going out the door. The door closes.

Our family had often visited theirs at the farm. A photo shows Margaret, with her parents and siblings, my sister and I with our mother, and several cousins. We're lined up, with a car in the background. Margaret's mother is holding a cake. It must have been a celebration for someone. Dudley wasn't there; probably he was napping, or with our father. Dad isn't in the picture — he would have been the photographer.

Contacts with this extended family continued while our mother fought cancer. Margaret or her sister came to our house on various weekends to provide help. The contacts continued after our mother died, becoming closer and deeper than I realized at the time.

On one visit to the farm, I had noticed a clue to Margaret and Dad's relationship. This visit was likely on a weekend, or during Easter vacation just before Dad's Studebaker announcement. All three of us children were visiting Margaret and her parents, probably for the purpose of "getting to know each other better." We found our entertainment in trailing along during farm work: "picking" eggs in the hen house, "slopping" the hogs, "calling" the cows from the pasture at milking time.

This time, I hopped into the car with Margaret to drive down the farm's access road to the mailbox, fixed to a post at the county road, which led to Belgrade – the nearest town. Margaret opened the mailbox, sorted through mail, and began to sing a popular song: "Sweetheart, sweetheart, sweetheart . . . . " I was surprised at her light soprano voice, accurately on tune. But I didn't associate this letter with my father, even when Margaret reminded us that Dad would retrieve us for our return trip to Alden Drive. If I put two and two together at the time, it was in my gut but not acknowledged by my head.

Plans for the wedding proceeded outside my attention. I must have avoided asking questions to learn more, as other young girls might have done, in other circumstances, or with different personalities. Instead, I followed along as events unfolded, obedient and stoic. When the 1947 Memorial Day Weekend arrived, we journeyed to Crow River Lutheran Church for the ceremony, and then gathered with family at the farmhouse. I know this from remembering a photograph taken from a distance, not because I recollect the occasion. Grandma and Grandpa weren't there. Margaret was twenty-seven years old when she and Dad married. It was a few months after the Studebaker ride, when I'd been imprisoned in the car, hearing Dad's announcement. I don't know how Carol and Dudley had learned about their plans to marry; Dudley doesn't remember. We didn't talk about it at the time.

CHAPTER 14

Ducks

———

FOR A FEW WEEKS BEFORE we moved to the new house on Brookside Terrace, my grandparents' yard hosted three ducks – survivors of my sister's care and Grandpa's hasty attention. Carol's birthday was in May. Inspired by Easter ads, I had purchased three ducklings and presented them to her in a cardboard carton, complete with saucers for water and food. Dad must have given permission. He was always enthusiastic about learning opportunities – we could learn some biology while observing them! Besides, we would move, in a month, to a house with a creek. Perhaps Dad used that fact to persuade my grandparents, if that was necessary. After all, they'd kept a cow for years during the twenties. Or, he might have thought these new "pets" would ease our transition to life with Margaret.

As we placed the carton with its three fluffy ducklings in our bedroom, I reminded Carol of the salesman's instructions: "Don't take them into the bathtub because they don't have feathers yet, and soap will hurt them."

She did it anyway.

I was reading in bed that night when something alerted me: I couldn't hear their constant cheeping. I got out of bed to check, and found the three hatchlings huddled together in a corner of their box. My sister was still in her bath. "Did you play with them in the bathtub?" She looked at me with a satisfied smile. "I told you not to do that. They're all cold and shivery." I ran downstairs to get help.

My grandparents must have been in the living room enjoying bedtime milk or coffee – Dad wasn't there – because the next thing I recall is Grandpa's moving into the kitchen as he tightened the fringed belt on his robe, his pajama legs brushing his leather slippers. He rummaged in the cupboards and stood in front of the stove as he lit the gas flame. Then he placed the ducklings in a sieve. He bounced them up and down over the flame, much as I bounce broccoli over the sink while rinsing it. Only, he did it forever. At last we put the dry ducklings into their box, said goodnight, and I took them upstairs.

One of the downy birds developed blisters on her feet; these popped soon after and left holes in the webs, although her swimming wasn't hampered. She walked with a limp because one hip had been injured, and we named her "Waddles." She attached herself to us – we must have become imprinted on her tiny brain as "mom." She followed us around with gentle quacking noises, leading the other two nameless birds in single file. The ducklings grew, discovered Grandma's little pond with its water lilies, and ate them all.

Grandma banished Waddles and company. We had to put them into a cardboard box, carry them a few blocks to the car line, board the streetcar with our cargo, and ride to the Brookside Terrace stop, as bemused passengers watched. Then we deposited our pets in the backyard. In June the moving van delivered our furniture and we moved in.

One warm October day I came home from school to see Waddles in the garden walking in circles, head bobbing to the left, and making giggle-noises. She greeted me, fell over, got up, and limped around in a zigzag way. She was drunk. In foraging for bugs, Waddles had uncovered and eaten apple peels, which fermented after Dad dug them into the garden soil. The other two ducks weren't affected. After awhile, Waddles sobered up and regained her place as head of the line.

Early one morning in late winter, my father awakened us with bad news: loose neighborhood dogs had attacked and killed the three ducks. He didn't want us to see feathers scattered on the bloody snow, but I glimpsed part of the ugliness as I left on my way to school. I missed the ducks for a while, but quickly transferred affection to the new pet, "Heinz" the dog, so named because he was a mongrel. We joked that he reminded us of the advertisement for Heinz soup: "57 Varieties."

Ducks remained part of the homestead, however, for years. Each spring, Margaret and Dad purchased a few, introduced them to the creek, fed them corn, and sometimes found an egg or two. Each fall, Margaret slaughtered them, cleaned them, and gave them to family and friends at holiday time. Margaret was a farmer's daughter who felt no personal attachment to poultry.

She was fierce, however, in protecting their investment. She told me years later that frantic quacking awakened her one morning. She rushed to the window, ran downstairs, and out the door in her nightgown. She pulled the canoe into the creek, climbed in, took a paddle and batted at a snapping turtle trying to capture the duck. I don't understand why the canoe didn't capsize. She forced the turtle to release the duck's leg, carried the rescued bird to the top of the slope, and set it free.

In Dudley's memory of the incident, it was Dad who rescued the duck with the turtle still attached. He beheaded the turtle; its head continued to snap on the lawn. Margaret and Dad removed the meat, sliced it, cooked it, and served it in cream sauce over toast.

Their ducks must be protected, because not even snapping turtles should jeopardize Margaret's presenting an oven-ready duck to neighbors. It was her way of being generous, of saying "thank you" to neighbors and friends.

CHAPTER 15

The Park on Brookside Terrace

———

THE NEW HOUSE AT 4437 Brookside Terrace was just over the village line in Edina, a mile and one-half from our grandparents' home. Its proximity meant Dad could stay there off and on ahead of time, to get it ready for moving in. It was a stucco house, built in 1912 on top of a hill, with a screen porch in front. From the porch we saw Minnehaha Creek flowing at the hill's bottom. The yard backed up to an unpaved road running alongside a railroad track, an undesirable feature that meant we could afford the house and yard. Even so, Dad had scraped for every penny of the down payment. During World War II, this trunk line had been used to ship munitions to the navigable part of the Mississippi River. The realtor assured Dad that because of the war's end, the track would be torn out. More than sixty years after we moved in, freight trains continue to travel through the neighborhood.

There was no street in front. The half-acre property faced directly onto the creek, which was wide enough for winter ice-skating circles, deep enough for summer canoes, and large enough to be labeled a river, were it flowing in New England. This running water made the property appealing in spite of railroad tracks. A level place alongside the creek looks like the remnant of a towpath alongside the current, moving south to the millpond, once the site of a gristmill. (Of course Grandpa had written about the miller George Craik in his column, "Parsonalities.")

Even at purchase time, the half-acre looked like a park. Two blue spruce trees framed the back of the house; nearby, an apple and a plum tree were already mature; in front stood two black walnut trees. Cattails bordered the creek, sheltering red-winged blackbirds with their "chirr" calls. A tall cottonwood tree on its banks threw shadows onto the moving waters.

Margaret and Dad plunged in together to turn house and yard into their home. Because we moved at the beginning of summer, they gave priority to the vegetable garden. A large plot – my guess is thirty by forty feet – was rototilled and planted. Every day was a battle day against weeds, bugs, rabbits, squirrels, and birds. The garden and preserving its harvest took time. Food not eaten immediately became juice, tomato sauce, canned apples, frozen vegetables, or jam.

One day during that first summer, Margaret asked me to give back-up help with the flower garden so she could work with vegetables. She told me to weed a flowerbed. Other than dandelions, I didn't know what a weed looked like. "If they're not growing in rows, or don't look like these, then it's a weed. These others are weeds." She pointed to some green things, but as soon as she left I could no longer distinguish them from other growth. I worked hard. I was diligent in pulling up and discarding many different-looking plants. When she came back to check on me, it turned out I'd pulled up her perennials, which are not planted in rows. Her voice became loud, her gestures jabbing. "Those aren't weeds! Look here. *That* one's a weed! *Oh, never mind.*" And she dismissed me. After that, all my chores were inside the house.

If only I had told her, many years later, that when my own young family moved into our first home, I faithfully watered a rapidly growing plant. Only after it was bushy, and taller than I was, did I ask myself what this plant might be. I hadn't seen it just a month beforehand. When I pulled it up, it was so shallow-rooted that it came up easily. It was a weed. It took another fifteen years for me to develop a fondness for gardening.

When their garden became fully developed, there was food in every season. Lettuce, peas, strawberries, and asparagus matured first. Then came green beans and rhubarb. Tomatoes, currants, gooseberries, and sweet corn flourished next. Pumpkins, squash and potatoes ushered in the fall. This was primarily Margaret's work – I've often thought of her as a farmer's daughter who now had her own place to "farm." But Dad was involved, too, after suppertime in the longer spring evenings, but mostly on weekends and during his summer vacation.

Once the garden was put to bed and food preserving completed, Dad and Margaret worked inside. Their first project involved stripping wallpaper, knocking out pillars that divided living room from dining room, applying a textured paint to cover plaster cracks, and more painting. Dad installed insulating tiles as a ceiling to lower heating costs. From the time we moved in, until well after my graduation from college, improvement projects were underway.

Margaret had always been high-energy; awake early, and hard at work before we children got up for school. But she became pregnant immediately and lived with nausea, so the work involved in making their new home depleted her. She did her best, but became overwhelmed as months went on. "I don't know what we'll have for supper," she often said. She sometimes sent Carol off on her bike just before supper, to buy a few cans of spaghetti-o's. She dashed about to prepare food – always at the last minute, it seemed. She shouted out exasperated instructions to Carol and me for setting the table or peeling potatoes. She would start to cook potatoes, leave the kitchen to attend to something, and then return with feet pounding down the hallway. So much was being juggled that each room filled with tension. There was no space to question or chat. Leisurely conversations – if any – took place between Margaret and Dad when we children weren't around.

Dad wasn't present to witness this whirlwind, for his long commute and late arrival for supper cushioned him. But one Saturday we gathered around the table for lunch, as we usually did. Dad was sitting with his back to the living room, I was on his left, and Margaret sat opposite him with ready access to the kitchen. My two siblings were opposite me – this was before Rolf and James were born.

Carol, Dudley, and I had been angry at each other, and brought our quarrel to the table. An insult was stated. A nasty retort followed. An accusation was hurled. A kick under the table was probably added. The pitch of our voices became higher as we ignored demands that we stop.

Then Dad pushed back his chair, placed his hand under his soup bowl, and turned it over.

Noodles slithered across the table and onto the floor. Chicken broth flowed in several directions. Tiny chunks of chicken settled in the rivulets. Everyone was quiet. For a moment, no one moved, except Dad. He was crying behind his fogged glasses, his high forehead bent over the table. He said something and left for his workshop. I was too shocked to hear what he said. Margaret followed him. Carol and I mopped up. When Margaret returned, she told us only that Dad was taking a break. We finished lunch and took our dishes into the kitchen. That was the only time I saw Dad so upset that his feelings surfaced in startling behavior. This newly formed, tension-ridden family was far from what Dad had anticipated.

I don't think that cooking interested Margaret. Eating was for refueling. I think she expected Carol and me to be more like farm girls with whom she grew up, or who were friends' daughters. An overheard phone conversation – Margaret was speaking – revealed this to me: "That girl! She can change a diaper and get the baby's food ready. She's one hard worker! I heard she made pot roast for the men when they were haying. And she's only thirteen." Girls like that had learned, while young, that they must weed in the kitchen garden and help cook a meal for the harvest crew. Those were girls already trained. Like Margaret herself. But not like Carol and me.

Grandma hadn't neglected to "train" me. (I don't know what Carol might have learned from her.) She had taught me how to clean toilets, wipe down the hardwood stairs, set the table, and iron linens. But Grandma had taken care of grocery shopping and cooking. And Margaret seemed to expect us to know things we hadn't learned. After all, she was inexperienced in first-hand communication with children – I understood this later.

I associate family with cooking and eating together: conversation, comfort food, various tastes, enjoying each other's company. It's the whole experience that nourishes. I felt this way when living with my grandparents. But Margaret couldn't do this. Her kind of cooking was necessary for the heavy work of farming or working in the garden. It didn't seem to be cooking as pleasure, experiment, or for a new taste sensation. Dudley has been more appreciative, remarking that Margaret managed good meals on a tight budget – he cited Sunday dinners such as beef tongue. I agree that tongue is delicious, but stronger in my memory is the family's sharing one chicken – eight of us, later on – ("Who wants the wing? Who wants the back?" my father asked cheerfully). But to me, family meals felt lean, not the abundant harvest meals of my grandparents' home. If there were routines, it didn't feel like it. It felt like disorganization – ferment with no strong center.

When company came or when we celebrated holidays, we trotted out the "universal holiday menu:" roast turkey, green beans, mashed potatoes, and ambrosia (canned fruit cocktail, canned peaches, canned pineapple, fresh apple chunks, marshmallows, and shredded coconut in a mayonnaise and whipped cream dressing). At Christmas we added lefse (a Norwegian flat bread),

Julebord, and pickled herring. At Easter we substituted ham for turkey. That menu was so embedded in the *idea* of holiday that when we five children planned a celebration of Margaret and Dad's fortieth wedding anniversary, the "universal menu" was what Margaret chose for the reception at church. After the gathering, relatives joined us at Brookside Terrace, and we served the same food all over again.

Even though Carol and I disappointed her, Margaret showed caring consideration for older neighbors, wherever she was. Many years later, she worked hard to get an elevator into our church so older members could get to the sanctuary. She also enjoyed young children. It was the late fifties, I think, when she joined the staff of a nursery school in our home church. She introduced preschoolers to experiences foreign to suburban children, such as field trips to farms. But she refused to get training in early childhood education because, after going to one class, she concluded "they just talk about ideas and can't tell you anything new." Certified teachers were included on staff, and Margaret remained as a strong figure in the background.

I'll always associate Margaret and Dad with making the Brookside Terrace "park" into a beautiful spot. It was their home. But it wasn't mine, as my grandparents' home had been. The move to Brookside Terrace altered the climate in my world. There were many changes yet to come – one after another to be weathered. At the time, who could have predicted all the events? They seemed to go on forever but were compressed within five years: a teachers' strike, two new family members, my grandmother's death, Grandpa's joining us, his political views, and his death – each one adding to the impact.

CHAPTER 16

Turbulence

———

AFTER WE MOVED IN THAT summer of 1947, I began eighth grade at Wooddale School in Edina. I loved learning, but eighth grade was painful. As long as I'd lived in Morningside, I felt at home – everyone knew my grandparents and Dad, who had grown up on Alden Drive.

In Edina, I felt lost as I watched groups of girls giggling together about their "New Look" with its longer skirts and layered petticoats. This postwar style, introduced in Paris early in the year, featured yards of material in multiple layers. Fashion designers had turned their backs on the frugal, tailored fashions of World War II. I had two hand-me-down dresses, which a relative had passed on at the last minute. I wore these on alternate days until I received more hand-me-downs. Eventually I saved enough baby-sitting money (at twenty-five cents an hour) to buy a plaid skirt with pleats, and a brown twin set.

My first proud purchase, however, had been a record album. It was a warm fall day when I boarded the streetcar at 44th Street and Brookside Avenue, transferred on France Avenue, and arrived at Lake Street. It didn't take long to find the record store, and locate the 78-rpm album I wanted. I returned home carrying the shopping bag through the kitchen, into the hallway, and out to the front screened porch. There stood the wind-up Victrola in its temporary place. I opened the album, removed the first record and began to listen to "Swan Lake."

Margaret heard the music, hustled through the door, and stood next to me. Her body was tensed. "*Listen!* You shouldn't be spending your money this way. We don't have any money for clothes for you. If you want clothes, you'll have to buy them yourself."

No one had said anything to me about this. Grandma had seen to it that we three had adequate clothing, by sewing or purchasing it. While our grandparents were always thrifty, there wasn't a feeling of scarcity. None of us had a large wardrobe, but skirts, dresses, or pants were there.

Buying a house and moving had burdened the family budget. Money – even for basics – was hard to find. Dad hated to share hard news. He might have thought we knew that we lived from one paycheck to the next. Perhaps he wanted to believe funds would become available, just as soon as a few bills were paid. There weren't family conferences around the table to discuss budget, as current parenting books advise. Margaret was upset and tense about making ends meet. Nor did she know how to describe the situation graciously.

Bad news did its work. After that moment on the porch, I always responded to baby-sitting jobs and bought my own clothing, although I don't think I paid for most shoes, boots, or coats.

When that first Christmas approached, Dad called the three of us into the living room. Carol, Dudley, and I stood in a semi-circle for his announcement. "Christmas is coming, and we're going to get a tree. But we can't afford decorations, so we'll make our own." We knew how to do this, so when the tree was set up in the living room, we used needle and thread to string cranberry-and-popcorn garlands, and made multi-colored construction paper chains.

Also, Dad presented a new idea with a lift in his voice: "We have some Ivory Snow Flakes, and with just a little bit of warm water and an egg beater we'll make snow flakes to decorate the branches." We delighted in taking turns with the hand beater, whipping up the broth into thick globs of "snow," which we applied to the branches. "Applying" soon became "throwing." Dad and Margaret were out of the room as we scooped up handfuls and hurled them at the tree. Ivory Snow Flakes missed the tree and landed on the wall, the table, and the rug. Dad's return and his "Stop it! Stop it, I say!" put an end to the mêlée.

I also connect that first year at Brookside Terrace with mud-covered overshoes. These were brown rubber "galoshes" with buckles, which closed a front flap. We were clumsy when walking because they were a large size, in order to cover our shoes. Since the road to the school bus stop wasn't paved, the spring thaw turned the walk into a mud soup hazard. My boots sank into the brown guck up to my ankles as I moved down the road and across the railroad tracks. A sucking sound accompanied each step as I scanned the mess for higher, solid ground. For weeks, it seems, I arrived at school with muddy overshoes, stowed them in my locker, and watched other students walk to their lockers with dry brown-and-white saddle shoes, or white bucks.

While I tried to cope with my misery by focusing on schoolwork and withdrawing into moodiness, tension increased in the family. Dad's participation in Union activities upped family anxiety. A strike was looming.

The Minneapolis Teachers Federation began its first strike on March 3, 1948, and Dad was in the picket line. Strikes never happen out of the blue. Dad had committed his evenings to take part in strategy meetings, as union members discussed terms and made phone calls to encourage fellow teachers to join the picket line. The Superintendent agreed that school employees needed a raise. But he was hampered because citizens had voted a cap on tax increases several years before. There were insufficient funds for educational needs. Mayor Hubert Humphrey said that under the circumstances, "Minneapolis is powerless" to provide enough money for a decent education. It was illegal for public employees to go on strike, but this didn't stop the Teachers Federation.

Margaret was eight months pregnant when the strike began. She must have been anxious and fearful, for we faced an unknown amount of time with no income. No doubt this contributed to her brittle responses when we children made a mess or failed to finish tasks she'd assigned.

One day after school, Dad asked us three children to come into the living room. He sat on the red couch as we took our places in several chairs. None of us expressed surprise at seeing him, although he was rarely home before suppertime. Margaret wasn't there. Dad cleared his throat before saying, "Margaret's been very tired, so she's gone to the hospital for a day or two, to get some rest."

We were silent. I felt surprised, but not worried, upset, or concerned about how we'd get along. I don't think there were plans for any other adult to pitch in and help. If Dad could make pancakes over a campfire, then we could heat up canned spaghetti. I suppose that after hearing this news we ate our supper, cleaned up, and went to bed.

The next evening, Dad assembled us again to say that Margaret would be returning the next day.

He broke our silence: "How are you feeling?"

Even in that moment, I recognized this as a startling question. Dad had never asked us about our feelings. He might have perceived our moods, or read our faces, and responded with action. He might have asked us what we *thought* about something. But he'd not asked us about feelings before – or since – that moment. I looked at the blue and red patterns in the oriental carpet, and responded, "Fine." Carol and Dudley shared similar monosyllables. "Good." "Okay." After this probe, it became quieter in the evening light. Then we all left the room.

Today I think Margaret had become so overwhelmed, frantic, and drained that she called Dad at work, and he took action. Maybe she requested hospitalization – she'd been a Nurse's Aide during the war, and knew that help was available. I suspect they had met with a physician or counselor, who heard about the family challenges, and suggested it would be helpful to share feelings. After that one try, we never again assembled for a family meeting. When Margaret returned, we took up our familiar habits, and coped.

One Saturday, Dad came home from the grocery store and asked me to help unpack staples. We went down into the basement where he bent over several cartons to rip them open with his pocketknife. We shelved their contents: canned corn, peas and "vegetable medley." These were the cheapest vegetables, which he'd purchased in quantity. Our canned and frozen garden produce was usually depleted by early winter, so we had to buy fruit and vegetables.

Throughout the strike we rotated through these cases: on the first night corn, the next peas, then "vegetable medley," and back to the corn. The corn sometimes appeared as "Squaw Corn," infamous in the family: open a can of creamed corn, plop it into a skillet with a "sclrop" sound, heat it, add a number of well-beaten eggs, scramble everything together, and dish up. (This Midwestern dish was a holdover from the Depression era. I'm sorry to say that we served Squaw Corn at suppertime even when there was no strike.)

My father's joining the picket lines raised fears for another reason: since he was now with "The Central Office," his loyalty was supposed to belong to the administration. I don't think the Superintendent threatened him with dismissal, but it was the McCarthy Era with its fear, blacklists, and capricious firing of public servants. Even with Dad's tenure, unemployment seemed possible. Although the strike was declared illegal in court, Dad participated in two more. The union won the right to collective bargaining after the third walkout. I'm sure Grandpa approved of Dad's carrying on the family legacy of working for justice.

Dad's participation in these strikes fed my feeling of isolation at school. None of my classmates had dads who walked picket lines. They seemed to be physicians, lawyers, and businessmen. In any case, we perceived them as comfortable or wealthy families. Today I feel proud of Dad's stand, but then I felt alone and embarrassed.

When the protest was over, work continued to engross Dad. He was developing the new Minneapolis Public Schools Audio-Visual Department: purchasing equipment, building a film library, training teachers, supervising staff, advocating for the budget. Each day he left for work early, energized, and returned home late, depleted. Although Margaret's mother came to help with the new baby Rolf, who was born at the end of March, she was needed at the farm. And Dad wasn't around much to keep things steady at home and counteract the ever-present tension.

I know that junior high school years can be miserable for many students. I know that sometimes each one feels as though she's the only one suffering. When I went through eighth grade, I didn't reflect upon, nor understand much about family dynamics. Instead, I just coped and groped through misery without being able to name my experience. But I did develop a few get-away strategies.

One day I walked to Grandma's house to see her. I wanted to be there with her, and she seemed surprised but happy to see me. I don't remember what we said or did. I think it was around the time of their planned trip to Mexico, when she had shared some Spanish words with me. Or she might have been getting ready to give a speech on behalf of the Women's International League for Peace and Freedom. Later she told Dad about my visit, who remarked – with a question in his voice – "Grandma said you went to see her yesterday."

"Yes."

He took in my response but didn't press for more information. That was his way. He never wanted to "intrude," he often said. Perhaps he feared what he might learn. Maybe Dad was already concerned, for he knew I wasn't thriving. A regular check up at the pediatric clinic had revealed I was losing weight, or at least not gaining. When I felt tense or upset, it settled in my gut. Food wasn't appealing; I didn't feel like eating. I suppose I'd responded to Dad's marriage, to the new living quarters, and to the atmosphere – frenetic in comparison to my grandparents' style – by withdrawing, and eating less. Dad and Margaret responded by purchasing a blender, and arranged for me to drink eggnog every night before bed. I made these myself after an easy lesson: whole milk, sugar, a raw egg, and nutmeg whipped into a frothy drink that tasted good. As far as I know, I gained weight after that, because the evening eggnogs stopped.

The Minneapolis Public Library was another escape – I went there once or twice a week after school. "I'm going to the library," I'd say to Margaret.

"Okay," in a flat voice.

I could tell she wasn't thrilled. Probably she wanted me to help her with ironing, or childcare. But who could object to my going to a library after school?

The Morningside Library was within walking distance; the city library (my choice) was a forty-minute ride on two streetcars. I entered the adult section, selected a novel, and read it in a leather chair under a window and in front of the radiator. During the winter, the radiator hissed behind me as it kept me warm. A favorite novel, which I read several times, was the story of a young city woman who married a Montana rancher and had difficult adjustments to make. The young woman's move into ranch life was a move into an alien environment, as strange as my setting was to me. One of the librarians came to recognize me and once approached me with another book in hand, suggesting it was more appropriate for my age. I thanked her, but checked out my favorite again.

It was a hard time for Carol as well, but we didn't know how to talk with, or support each other. Carol seemed like an easier, happier person than I was. I didn't know that *she* didn't feel nurtured until years later when she told me about her paper route. At the time, a paper carrier had to collect the subscription money from each customer. Some customers turned her away, saying "we don't have the money now." When she received the bill, she covered it with her own money, without being repaid. Because she wasn't confident she could receive help from Margaret and Dad, she didn't ask. They probably assumed everything was just fine.

Maybe all adolescents want to escape. Yet, when I reflect on that time, it still feels chaotic. I didn't know how to respond, except to dream in my room about an unknown boyfriend-to-be who would look like the movie star Cornel Wilde. I did schoolwork, attempted to learn French by myself, went to the library, took babysitting jobs, and read. I tried for competence at school, and worked at household chores: ironing, dishes, and cleaning. Eventually, I made two friends, but that was later.

It was a long time before I looked at those years at Brookside Terrace honestly and recognized that Dad and Margaret hadn't provided emotional support throughout the transition from Alden Drive to Brookside Terrace, from one family configuration to another. Margaret knew how to nurture plants, but not Dudley, Carol, or me. Neither Dad nor Margaret was warm in temperament, and both were action oriented, as I now tend to be. We weren't a family that sat around a table and talked, as I recall my grandparents doing. We didn't feel free to ask questions, or raise concerns (unless it was about a math problem, or science homework, with which Dad was always eager to help). Margaret and Dad didn't create opportunity for "talking things over." Either they didn't know how, or were too harassed to find the energy.

Now that I'm no longer that adolescent, it's obvious that twenty-seven years was young for Margaret to be presented with three children, twelve, ten and eight years old. She did her best, but had too much to manage. Who wouldn't be overwhelmed, as she was? I think everyone in the family just coped. When change comes, so does anxiety. A family leader can marshal strengths in response to difficulties. But too many challenges can become a bad weather front, sweeping away sunny days. We went through chaos because it was so hard to deal with the pile-up of changes. Nurture was in short supply.

As a result of that time, perhaps *because* of that turbulence, we children also gained positive values: we never felt entitled, we were resourceful, we knew many teachers and church leaders who cared, and we loved learning. We knew that our grandparents and parents worked to make things better for others in our society.

And we learned to make homemade decorations for a Christmas tree.

CHAPTER 17
Discovery

———

"OH! THAT'S WHY I HATE her!"

This insight stopped me when I was sixteen. I don't know if I was studying in my room, or setting the dining room table; whether I was standing or sitting; if it was daylight or twilight. I do know that understanding was swift. It capped a memory.

The recollection had burst into my conscious thought. What released it from its hiding place? What nudged, shoved, pushed it into view, so I could use it? The prod is lost.

My recall was visual. I saw my eleven-year-old-self as if it were happening to someone else, to a young girl in a home movie, with action slowed down.

Her father's desk was oak, stained dark, a classical teacher's desk. The mat holding the eighteen by twenty-four-inch blotter aligned with the desk's long edge. His T-Square and slide rule lay above the mat, parallel with it. At the blotter's upper right corner, an inkwell sat on an inlaid tray from India. Next to that was the brass ashtray, with four dimples in the circular rim for holding burning cigarettes. At the far right edge was the device for rolling his own smokes.

A long drawer held pens, compasses, and other tools for a math and science teacher. Under that drawer, the kneehole. Next to the kneehole, a door. It opened onto a larger storage space, maybe intended for books or graph paper.

She was drawn to this storage space, this one time, without knowing why. It must have been at the end of summer, when her grandmother was busy picking corn and tomatoes for supper. The house held no activity except for hers. She entered her father's bedroom, sat on the oriental carpet, and opened the desk's door.

Several bundles of envelopes were piled there. Square-ish blue envelopes. Tissue-like paper. Real stationery, not school-tablet paper. Held together with rubber bands. Addressed to her father.

She opened an envelope and pulled out the letter. She read "Dearest Dudley." She felt quickened, realizing she'd found love letters. She looked again at the bundles, started to count the envelopes, then picked up the opened letter again. She hesitated for a second. Her first thought wasn't about violating privacy, but about satisfying curiosity. She felt intrigued, as would any eleven-year-old. She read on. There was something about "that day at the lake." Nothing more specific. Which lake? What had happened? Why was it important? The signature was Margaret's.

She returned it to the envelope, and opened another "Dearest Dudley." This one referred to a response: "You say it's not time, and we should wait." Wait for what? Wait to do what?

She opened the third letter, sped past the greeting, and read, "I heard that Luella died – I'm sorry." She reread the sentence, returned the letter to the envelope, and re-opened the first letter. She saw the date. It had been written before her mother died.

Margaret and her father had loved each other while her mother was ill, and still alive.

She moved quickly to re-bundle the envelopes. She wondered what time it was. She hadn't heard a door open. Her grandmother must still be outside. But she worried that she'd be found out. She left the room.

I had buried this memory for five years. Something had snapped shut. It was a clean cut-off. It wasn't present on the day Dad took me for the Studebaker ride, to announce that he and Margaret would be married. It wasn't there at the wedding. It didn't show up when we were moving.

"Oh! No wonder I hate her!" This self-understanding began to free me. My mind began to see my turmoil. Something calmed down. Slowly, I became more cooperative in the family. I disappeared less frequently when needed for household help. I didn't snap so much at Margaret. I followed through on promises. It was still difficult to be in the same household, and I still felt as though I belonged to Grandma. But my attitude began a slow change, and this change became ground for softness toward Margaret years later.

When my own children were adults, I had another insight: *I don't have to refer to her as my mother. She's my stepmother.* I asked myself: *If she were a member of a church you serve, what would you say about her?* My response: *You'd say, "She's an interesting character."* After that, I enjoyed talking with her each week, listening to her weather reports, and hearing stories about distant relatives. I could let her be herself.

When Dad lay dying in 1996, I had lunch with my siblings in the hospital grill and told them about discovering the letters. I hadn't told anyone before that moment, for it felt like a family secret that had to be kept. My siblings, friends, and I hadn't shared stories like that – I suppose I hadn't trusted anyone with heavy information. Nor do I know what prompted me to share during that lunchtime. Possibly Dad's impending death meant I wouldn't have to acknowledge my discovery to him.

My brothers and sisters received this news calmly and without comment. No surprise expressed, no shocked statements, no questions of curiosity, no probing of my feelings, no words of wonder. Dad's dying and the need to talk about Margaret's next steps overshadowed everything. We returned to our hamburgers, musing about Dad's deterioration, the twenty-below weather, and starting our cars every hour to avoid battery death. Minnesotans discuss weather to avoid talking about feelings.

It was the wrong time to tell Dad or Margaret how I'd snooped into their mail fifty years earlier. I didn't need to. I didn't feel alienated from them, nor that I must bridge a chasm of misunderstanding, nor that saying anything would help anyone. I didn't broach the subject again.

Family members have observed that women pursued Dad, not the other way around. He said as much, in one of his letters to my mother Luella, before they married. I discern Dad's reticence, too, in reading two years' worth of my parents' letters before they decided to marry – my mother seemed more ardent than he. She expressed feelings more easily.

Dudley has said that our mother chose Margaret as her replacement. He hasn't given a reason, but I suppose it's possible. She had felt affection for Margaret. An early picture shows Margaret with her arm draped around Mother's shoulder, my mother's arm around Margaret's waist. Standing next to them is Katherine, Margaret's sister. Sitting below the group is Clara – our mother's first cousin – who was Margaret and Katherine's mother.

There's another reason Dudley's speculation could be true. When my mother knew her illness was terminal, she wrote to her friend expressing worry about us three children: "Of course I want Dudley to re-marry as soon as possible, but what decent woman would want 3 small kids."

I'll never know whether my mother did choose a replacement. But I believe now, as I have during rare conversations with siblings, that there had been a mysterious mixture of Dad's passive charm, Margaret's attraction to him, and a need to care for three children. I believe theirs was a romantic love, an emotional affair, not fully physical, when those discovered letters were written. I'll never know the balance of pursuit and response. That balance doesn't matter now.

CHAPTER 18

Camel Cigarettes, Apricot Chair, Shakespeare

——

OUR LEAVING ALDEN DRIVE FOR Brookside Terrace must have been an adjustment for my grandparents, too. They had gained more freedom: less food to cook, more time to read, easier household cleaning, more socializing, plenty of time to garden. They had more physical and emotional space, and a return to cherished routines. Grandpa could sit in his chair in the quiet evening, poring over his *Atlas* again, reading the latest history book, or scribbling out a verse on used envelopes. Grandma could work on a tablecloth with her crochet hook, or darn a sock. Together they'd listen to music on the radio without our restless interruptions. But I imagine these benefits were mixed with a sense of loss. That's what I feel when I can't see my grandchildren.

They didn't have much time to enjoy their regained space. Eighteen months after movers loaded the truck for Brookside Terrace, Grandma suffered a stroke. She arose early and toppled over in the bathroom. Grandpa rushed to her, somehow got her into bed, and called their physician. I suppose there was a hospital stay, but I doubt that a rehab program followed. Instead, there was advice to rest, avoid tension, and hope for improvement.

After this shock to the system (both hers and our family system), she went to bed early, woke late, and took longer naps. Somehow she recovered enough for garbled speech and slow housework. Grandpa took over most of the cooking and cleaning. One day he made some muffins for her; I was there when he interrupted himself "Oh! I forgot baking powder." He opened the oven door, removed the muffins, poked a hole in each top and sprinkled a bit of the powder into each one. He asserted later, "They tasted just fine."

I'm sure Margaret and Dad pitched in, as well as taking care of three older children, one-year-old Rolf, and the always-necessary vegetable garden.

Grandpa expressed his grief on the flyleaf of his *Encyclopedia Britannica Atlas*. But even then, he couldn't contain his political interests.

> It's been a long time since I entered remarks – a time
> during which Clara has been steadily growing weaker.
> Her seizures come nearly every day now with pains
> in the chest and left arm and foot and an almost im-
> possible breathing. She has taken nitro-glycerin pills,
> digitalis and aromatic spirits of ammonia regularly.
>
> And since August the war against Korea has gone
> on apace. The allied forces (mostly United States)
> pushed the Koreans back almost by Christmas. And
> then appeared some half-million Chinese soldiers
> who at this writing are recovering for the Koreans
> their lost nation. In the meantime the U.N. is strug-
> gling to solve the problems created by the fighting.[35]

Grandma was told to stop smoking, but she defied instructions. When we visited, Carol later told me, Grandma sent her to the drugstore on France Avenue with orders to return with a pack of Camels. I don't know if Grandma tried to hide her forbidden hab-it, or if her defiance was open.

We continued to include our grandparents at Sunday meals, so Dad drove the Studebaker to Alden Drive after church and returned with them to Brookside Terrace for the afternoon. They inspected the vegetable garden as they moved slowly from the driveway past the corn, green beans, and apple tree, to arrive at the door opposite the ferns, cleome, and cosmos. Grandma always looked well put together and cared for, as the lady she was, with her powdered face and white hair piled on top of her head. But her appearance disguised her frail body. After dinner it was painful to observe her failing health: the tortured walk back to the car, the rapid breathing, the mewing sounds of pain, the nitroglycerin under her tongue, the blessed quiet of relief. She survived this way for two and one-half years.

The phone call came one morning when I was sixteen years old. She had died of a second stroke, which occurred in the same manner as the first: early in the morning, in the bathroom, toppling over. When I arrived downstairs for breakfast, I heard the news. It was a perfect June day – outside.

I asked Margaret if I could go to my grandparents' house to "do something." She sensed that I needed to work. I could see her searching for ideas, and when she suggested I clean in their home, I left at once. After walking to Alden Drive, I entered a silent house. Grandpa must have been meeting with the minister or the funeral director. I began to work, alone. I concentrated on the living room, getting down on my knees to clean around the rug. I took the dust cloth and lifted the edge of the rug to remove grit from the hardwood floor, as Grandma had taught me. A neighbor rang the bell to drop off food for my grandfather. I rose to greet her, received the offering, and thanked her. Later, I got the report that I'd been very grown up, for a sixteen-year-old. I did feel like a contributing adult while dusting and vacuuming.

The living room at 4210 Alden Drive held no more family gatherings. I thought I'd never see that room again, with its console radio, curved plaster fireplace and Grandma's apricot chair. The beige rug, and toile wallpaper populated with beige shepherdesses sitting on hillocks, and holding beige crooks, was to disappear from my sight. It was in that room we had listened to "Duffy's Tavern" every week. (A telephone rings: "Duffy's Tavern, where the elite meet t'eat Duffy ain't here.") It was there she sat on the sofa and crocheted tablecloths I now use at Christmas time. Her teapot was on the tray, her cigarette dangled from her mouth. In that living room we read a Shakespeare play out loud, taking parts that Grandma assigned to us, because she had tickets to a performance and wanted to re-read the play. As I dusted and vacuumed I saw myself turning pages and reading dialogue.

Members of my wider family refer to the house on Brookside Terrace as "home." Perhaps they assume I feel as they do. It makes sense to them, for I lived there for nine years before leaving, and only three years at our grandparents' house. But Alden Drive was the place I loved, a home where I connected with Grandma and Grandpa. There, I still found a bridge to my mother. On that June day in 1951, I needed to be there, dusting and vacuuming, giving something to the house and to my grandparents, who had nurtured me.

Aunt Peg and Uncle Edgar drove with three-year-old Polly, all day and all night, from Washington D.C. for the funeral. At the time, it was common practice to have open caskets during funeral services. Soon after the benediction, the minister sought me out and took me to see Grandma lying there. I stood briefly, looking at her. Her hands were crossed over her burgundy crepe dress – the one she always wore when she gave speeches in the cause of peace. Her face was powdered. Her rimless glasses were on. She was still a lady. "She is at peace," the minister said. I nodded.

But I wasn't at peace. Her death had brought me to a mighty pause.

The change from Alden Drive to Brookside Terrace had been a shock to my system. Where once there had been order, routines, and expectations, now there was confusion and disorder. It was like moving to a foreign country where the words sounded familiar but the meaning had changed. As long as Grandma lived, I could think of her home as a refuge, a place I understood, a place where I felt understood. Now that she was dead, my world was unsteady. I couldn't name my feelings at the time, but I begin to get it now.

Grandma had been over 65 when my father, and the three of us children, all under the age of ten, moved into their home in 1944. Now that I'm over 65, and recall engaging with my own grandchildren before they were ten, I'm aware of the energy she used on our behalf. For years I felt – without recognizing the feeling – that she had spent her vitality, so I was responsible for her death. Such guilt isn't unusual, I realize, but it was present as an unacknowledged weight.

The burden was lifted one night when I was middle-aged. I had awakened at two a.m. and couldn't return to sleep. I got up and put on my bathrobe. The house was quiet and cool. I went into the study, turned on the desk lamp and closed the door. I needed to discover what was bothering me. I opened my journal and began to write. The words poured out – I don't know what they were, exactly, but I began to recall my sixteen-year-old self on my knees, dusting the floor in another silent house. Then a new sentence stared back at me: "I did not cause her death." I hadn't recognized I'd been carrying this feeling, until seeing my own words on paper.

Within a month of Grandma's death, Grandpa sold 4210 Alden Drive and moved in with us. He wasn't able to maintain his home with his income, and it was logical that he, Margaret, and Dad consolidate resources. The move added to his grief for Grandma. She had shared many of his ideals. She was politically active as a speaker for the Women's International League for Peace and Freedom, an organization that aroused suspicion during the McCarthy era. But she probably tempered Grandpa's idealism with her practical sense, and he must have lacked tether in the new surroundings at Brookside Terrace, just as I did.

"As soon as I could do so after Clara's death," Grandpa wrote in the margins of his Atlas, "I went to [Britain] and Italy." He fled.

CHAPTER 19

Fresh Air

———

I WASN'T AROUND WHEN GRANDPA sold the Alden Drive house, nor when James was born at the end of July. Instead, I was on a two or three week visit with Aunt Peg, Uncle Edgar, and Polly in Washington, D.C.

They had invited me to return with them right after Grandma's funeral. The weeks preceding Grandma's death had been difficult – seeing her limited capacity, waiting for further deterioration, Margaret and Dad's giving extra help to Grandpa. It was even harder for Margaret, who was nauseous throughout her pregnancy. So I suspect Dad and Margaret welcomed Peg and Ed's invitation to me. I'd be one less person for them to think about. I was happy to be invited, too. Peg and Ed brought zest with them – a visit in their home promised fun.

With my packed suitcase, I got into my aunt and uncle's car with whitewall tires, which Peg and Ed had cleaned with Bab-O scouring powder the day before. The first leg of our trip was about an eight hours' drive to Milwaukee, Wisconsin, where we planned to stay overnight with Peg's niece. When we pulled up to the curb and left the car at last, we were startled to find the can of Bab-O sitting upright on the front bumper, where Peg had put it down temporarily. Their car had perfect aerodynamics!

Throughout the journey, I rode in the back seat with three-year-old Polly. When it came time for Polly's nap each afternoon at

2 o'clock, I moved into the front seat (there were no bucket seats), and my young cousin spread out in the back. Except for that one hour of sleeping, it seemed to me that Polly talked for the entire three-day trip. Now I'm happy whenever Polly and I can chatter; her outgoing nature helps me keep connected.

In their part of the family, there was conversation. I didn't understand, at the time, that my aunt and uncle were re-introducing me to a style of seeking and expressing opinion, differing with others, and evaluating experiences: Peg didn't like a restaurant lunch, which wasn't up to par; Ed was pleased with the choice of motel; we all wondered if a roadside historic marker was worth a quick stop.

When we arrived at their home in Chevy Chase, Maryland, their open style continued. Aunt Peg was a handsome woman whose hair had turned white early. It set off her bright red lips and blue eyes. She sparkled. She stated her expectations and opinions clearly: "Who used the last ice cube and didn't fill the tray?" Or, "Try this barbecue sauce – there's a taste bang for you!" She expressed feelings: "It's hard to live as far from family as we do, but we make the best of it by celebrating holidays with friends."

Uncle Edgar was a quieter person, who was warm, witty, and enjoyed punning. His puns were swift off his lips and vanished just as quickly, leaving us laughing but not recalling them. He learned that I was wondering about journalism as a career, since I enjoyed working on the high school newspaper. He read a story I'd written, said, "I like your crisp style," and took the trouble to connect me with a newspaper reporter whom he knew. This was a woman who took me out to lunch, and led me straight to reality: "If you want to work on a newspaper, you'll have to work in the Women's Section. There aren't career choices for women in the serious news sections. But if you begin with recipes and clothing, you might move up. Or you might not." I lost interest. I knew I'd be a disaster in fashion reporting, and testing recipes sounded more like majoring in Home Economics.

Both Peg and Ed traded opinions freely: "My mother was a difficult person."

"Oh, Ed, she was not! I adored your mother!"

"Oh, yes, she could be hard to live with."

"Ed, I adored her!"

Their home also felt orderly. We ate left-overs Friday night and cleaned the stove, worked around the house and garden on Saturday morning, sometimes had a barbecue Saturday evening, watched the comic Ernie Kovacs on television, and enjoyed Sunday dinner after church served on "the Spode," as we referred to the blue-patterned earthenware set. These experiences of openness and order now seem to be simple and normal approaches to family life, but then I observed them with wonder, keeping thoughts to myself. Nor did I understand that it might be easier to live in an orderly manner when only three or four people are involved.

Peg and Ed took me around to see major sites in Washington: the Mall, the Lincoln and Jefferson Memorials, the Capitol building, and Embassy Row. The monuments and buildings impressed me because of their elegant lines, rational designs, and stately settings. At the Lincoln Memorial, I felt touched in a deep place as I stood near Lincoln's chair and read his words carved on the walls. It moves me still, whenever I'm there. As we drove around the city, I also heard about frustrations with D.C. traffic circles, streets going off at odd angles, and that Washington, D.C. was truly a southern city. "Everyone's slow here. Everyone takes their time," was Peg's observation. She was enthusiastic about "the flowers in spring – the azaleas, the rhododendrons, the cherry blossoms all over the place!" They introduced me to exotic tastes, such as barbecue sauce, upside down cake, and seafood. (Since Margaret couldn't stand fish, the only time the rest of us ate it was when Dad cooked it while camping.)

But even with Peg and Ed's stimulating approach to various topics and their willingness to explore ideas, we never talked about Grandpa's strong leftist views. Were they embarrassed? I don't know. They knew it wasn't helpful to be pegged as such during the Cold War, when politicians, actors, and writers were vilified. No one wanted to be judged guilty by association – especially not in a father-son relationship. Nor did I ask. In all of the Parsons family, when it came to open discussion of Grandpa's politics, we in the younger generation intuitively knew *do not bring it up; do not cross this line.*

I treasure that time with Aunt Peg and Uncle Edgar. While with them, I breathed another atmosphere. Because they were family, there was enough in common with Dad so I could feel secure. Because they weren't my nuclear family, it was a comfortable way to experience difference.

But I couldn't stay for long in that summer of 1951. When the vacation was over, I boarded one train in Union Station, changed trains in Chicago, and returned home. I was refreshed, more secure as myself, and looked forward to seeing my friends Ronna and Sarah.

These two girls and I had developed friendships during the two previous years – my sophomore and junior years in high school. Ours were one-on-one relationships; the three of us didn't socialize as a group. Ronna was being raised in a comfortable home, but felt "other" in her environment, as I did in mine. She'd been adopted from a situation of poverty and neglect, and her mother was still alive. I think initial contact between the two families came through their church, and Ronna continued to see her mother on arranged visits. What did we talk about? Perhaps teachers, classes, and other students during the time we spent together after school, mostly at her house, and sometimes for sleepovers at each house.

My other friend was Jewish. Sarah also invited me to her home after school, and I often ended up staying with her family for the beginning of Shabbat. I loved being included in the ceremony of lighting Shabbat candles, and hearing the Friday evening prayer in Hebrew, before beginning dinner. I learned that Sarah's family was from upper New York State. ("It's not like New York City, Janet. It's a beautiful place," said Sarah's mother in response to my expression.) They must have been one of few Jewish families in Edina-Morningside. Through Sarah, I met other girls whom she knew through her Temple in Minneapolis. I was invited to services, and once joined the family for Yom Kippur, a great honor. I loved the ritual, with its orderly musical responses. For a while, I wished I were Jewish, too.

Why was that? Their families expressed opinions, and shared comments about friends, movies, boys, schools, and aspirations. What profession was this girl interested in? Would that boy be able to make it as a doctor? Why would anyone wear an outfit like that? They wove contributions like these throughout their lively, engaged conversations. Yet, there were no questions or comments about Grandpa, whose opinions were published in newspapers, and must have been known to at least a few of these families. Maybe they wanted to protect me from their responses. Perhaps they didn't even connect Grandpa and his letters with me.

Following an afternoon in environments like those, I returned home to activity without reflection: setting table, mashing potatoes, feeding snacks or a meal to younger brothers, waiting for Dad to arrive home so we could eat, scattering to clean up, washing dishes, attending to homework. During this set of jobs, Margaret put Rolf and James to bed. It's all we could manage.

Today, I feel fortunate that both my sons have smaller families, so they can take time to be with their children. They also have an open style. They seem to discuss a wide range of topics, from current events to sex. TV, the movies, and their friends provide fodder for questions and discussion, although I think religious faith is an uncomfortable subject for them.

But when I was a teenager, I stepped into breathing space through experiencing two different cultures – my Jewish friend and acquaintances, and my aunt and uncle's branch of the family. I realize now that part of any young person's growing up is being introduced to family styles differing from their own. In that respect, my experience wasn't unusual. And I suppose each family might have some topic to be avoided, decided by subconscious but mutual understanding. In ours, it was Grandpa's leftist take on ideal community.

CHAPTER 20

Grandpa's Flight

———

IN THE ATLAS WHERE HE had loved to browse and add his thoughts in its margins, Grandpa jotted his conviction about travel:

> "How beautiful upon the mountains are
> the feet of him that bringeth good tidings,
> that publisheth peace…" Isaiah 52.7
>   What are the "good tidings?" What, indeed, but
> the information that comes from much travel, if not
> in trains or airplanes then on magic carpets that,
> like Puck, can ring the world swiftly and surely. No
> honest traveler can ever be prejudiced against any
> people and can never want war upon a people.[36]

Shortly after moving in with us, Grandpa seized the day to travel again. At seventy-four, he still had his curiosity. He could escape into another world.

But before he took off, he was set up in the smallest bedroom. It had textured yellow-gold paint on the walls, and a curtain patterned in orange and brown that covered the closet's entrance – there wasn't room for a door to swing open. The only window provided a view of the back yard, blue spruce trees, vegetable garden, garage, and railroad track. A narrow bed, a dresser, and a desk occupied nearly all the space. My grandfather moved into these quarters from an ample house, yard, and neighborhood, where he had talked, worked, and ranged.

Carol and I used bunk beds in a larger room; three-year-old Rolf slept in its corner. Margaret, Dad, and the new baby Jim occupied the remaining large room. Dudley was moved into a tent on the side lawn – since he was a Boy Scout, Dad might have thought he'd like the adventure. I have no idea how we handled rainy nights – our WWII surplus tent was made of canvas. When rain was heavy, water pooled in the sagging top, saturated the canvas, and dripped onto the sleeping occupant. I hope Dudley slept on the living room couch during bad weather.

Those were our accommodations for eight people: one bathroom, three bedrooms, and a tent. The ducks stayed down at the creek, the dog slept outside in his house. And then there was the cat.

"Janet," Grandpa said to me, "I want to have a pet – a cat – but Margaret doesn't approve." He was standing in the doorway of his tiny room, having heard me climb upstairs to escape the clatter of supper preparation. He was impossible to resist, especially since he could be an ally against Margaret.

"I know someone with little kittens; they're looking for homes. I'll get one for you but you can't tell anyone I did this." Without hesitating, my upright grandfather agreed to lie, and soon I brought the kitten home, holding it inside my coat. I sneaked it into his room. He kept her there, hidden.

The day of discovery came.

"I want you to see this." Margaret pulled me aside and took me upstairs. She opened the door to Grandpa's room. "Look!"

She pointed to the newspapers on the floor, the food and water dishes, the litter box, the tiny white-nosed creature. "He says he found it on the street." Her voice conveyed skepticism, and I remained silent, watching her body tense up as she shut his door. "My mother never allowed cats in the house. They belong in the barn. Filthy creatures." We went downstairs. (Nearly sixty years later, she mentioned the incident and I confessed. She didn't seem surprised.)

Within six weeks of joining our household, Grandpa started his journey, Dudley slept indoors again, and somehow the kitten disappeared. Dad and Margaret had planned to expand the house with help from an architect cousin. They worked together to design the addition and supervise construction. The front screen porch was removed for two new rooms. Two back-to-back fireplaces were installed and faced with redwood boards. The front one opened to the living room.

On either side of that fireplace, two steps led down into the addition, part of which was Grandpa's room. It held the second fireplace, a bath with shower, bookshelves, and windows overlooking Minnehaha Creek through the shade of a tall spruce. The other steps led to a sunny entranceway. It provided space for Margaret's numerous houseplants and a coat tree, which stood alongside the front door for fifty-eight more years. Margaret and Dad now had a master bedroom on the second floor – its windows provided an audio-visual of the creek's duck flotilla.

Before long, we received postcards marking Grandpa's trail. I still have a few. A picture of the Cunard "Scythia," postmarked 16 August 1951 bears his ditty:

Is she not a gallant craft
Whether forward seen or aft
As she plows the waters green
Not a finer sight is seen
And the people that she bears
Sink within her all their cares.
We are having a fine time keeping busy with talk,
meals, movies, sleep, books and – thoughts keeping.

The second one, dated 13 September, depicts an airline flight path from Dublin to London.

> Our flight from Dublin to Bristol having been "indefinitely postponed" according to the announcer I am sitting here cooling my heels in the station. I came in from the rural area of Kells whence I went on Wednesday to make a connection with "The Book of Kells" that I saw in Trinity College Library, Tara home of ancient kings and other things. This morning I interviewed De Valera, president of Eire.
>
> Dad and Gramps[37]

"This morning I interviewed De Valera, president of Eire." *That's all he had to say about an appointment with the dominant political figure in Ireland!* Of course, this was written on a postcard; but he did summarize his meeting in a later report to the *Hennepin County Review:*

Ireland is Prosperous, Parsons Finds

E. Dudley Parsons is traveling in England, Scotland and Ireland. He has been visiting his numerous relatives in England, where he was born, and last week went to Dublin. His report reveals that Eire is prospering more than is generally believed on this side. Editor.

I called on Eamon De Valera one morning. He remembered some of the Irishmen of Minneapolis who had interested themselves in the independence movement that he led, especially Mr. John Gleason, of the Gleason Mortuary. Mr. De Valera had been in nearly all of the cities of the United States. He found himself much indisposed, he said, to give interviews and so I felt especially honored to be received.[38]

Grandpa described his stay in Italy in a long article. It's filled with anecdotes and observations about economic difficulties for laborers and farmers, land distribution, and the coming elections. He pushed forward to gain entrance to the offices of the Socialist and Communist parties. There he engaged in conversation, reporting that the two parties agreed on food and land distribution. But, he stated, their other divisions kept Prime Minister DeGasperi in office. And so he determined to interview DeGasperi, stubbornly acquiescing to a five-hour wait:

> DeGasperi will work as hard as he can to fill both of his positions efficiently. Refreshed by his visit to the United States, he is optimistic over the future of Italy. He is a very pleasant person to talk with, and does much better with English than do his clerks and secretaries who, though courteously, hurried me from palace to palace for five hours before I was let into the presence of the Prime Minister. As I had promised, I took only five minutes of his time, giving him greetings from his United States admirers and asking him but one question: "Do you think, Mr. DeGasperi, that your visit with Mr. Truman was successful?"
>
> "Yes, I believe so," he said. "I came away assured of the continued help of the United States in solving our problems."
>
> "But what of Trieste?" I asked.
>
> "We shall be able to settle that in friendliness, I feel sure. But we must not be too impatient."
>
> As I took my leave, I took with it an engaging smile and walked out of the great palace where the foreign office is located between meticulous soldiers who saluted me as though I had been a royal personage. Through marbled halls, out into a court and through this to the majestic front steps that are

almost washed by an ever spouting fountain, I came out into the gaiety of the evening, well lighted and full of color.[39]

Grandpa left Italy on October 16th, 1951 and reappeared in Edina in November, looking thinner. He moved into his new space in the completed addition, and took up his activities: writing, Saturday Lunch Club, gardening, and church. His flight after Grandma's death was a flight from Edina into political interests. He loved to travel. And he couldn't stop looking at the world politically.

CHAPTER 21

Compelled to Write

———

WHEN I WALKED THROUGH THE door of *The Hennepin County Review*, I was soon to be a high school senior and editor of the school paper, *The Buzzette*. Grandpa had found me a job. At least, that's probably how it began, because he knew Editor and Publisher James L. Markham, who published Grandpa's verse and his "Parsonalities" column in the *Review*.

One day in late summer just before he left for Europe, Grandpa told me to go to the newspaper office to speak with Mr. Markham. I'm sure his words were abrupt and direct: "You like writing, don't you? Go to the Hopkins newspaper. Markham's expecting you. There might be a job for you."

So I climbed aboard the streetcar at 44th Street and Brookside Avenue for the twenty-minute ride, which first went through a marsh with tall cattails and flitting blackbirds. After moving alongside suburban tract houses and through open spaces, I arrived in Hopkins proper, the business center for nearby raspberry fields, vegetable farms, and Minneapolis-Moline – a manufacturing company of tractors and other machinery.

I was surprised that the office of a real newspaper seemed so small. Now I imagine the front door's appearance: *Hennepin County Review/Hopkins, Minnesota*, written in bronze-colored letters. This door swung open to two desks on the left, perpendicular to the plate-glass window. One was to become mine, part of the time. As soon as I entered, someone led me straight ahead to the Editor's office and introduced us.

He might have been tall once – or never – but when I met him, he was bent over at the waist so that his body formed a right angle and his eyes looked at the floor. He had to raise his head to see where he was going, sweeping the room from left to right, as he limped forward, one hand on his left hip. He must have been born with this scoliosis. I assumed he'd aged into that posture, although I'd never met any older person who looked like that, and in fact he wasn't old at the time.

Mr. Markham showed me around. To the left of his office, we entered the pressroom, with its fragrance of ink, hot lead, and oily machinery. Right away I could see the linotype machine, which looked like an upright piano, only narrower and taller. The keyboard was like a typewriter's, except that it released tiny, hot lead letters into long chutes the width of a newspaper column. The operator of this machine read a story from the hand-written or typed copy, which hung from a hook at eye-level. As he typed, he had to figure out how to justify the margins, and couldn't make corrections. That came later, after the proofreading. "The next step," Mr. Markham pointed out, "is to place these columns into a frame, along with the ads and photos." When all was in place and the frame tightened, a proof was printed on long, continuous sheets of paper.

Editor Markham often called me into his office to help with proofreading. He read out loud in this manner: "Capital A after the vote was taken comma the Village capital V Council capital C went on to the next order of business period new paragraph capital T the next item under discussion proved to be contentious period." I marked the proof as I'd learned to do in journalism class: a mark in the margin to point out a needed correction in the line, then at the correct spot either three parallel lines for a capital letter, an "l.c." for "lower case" or a loop to indicate a deletion.

Sometimes it was my turn to read from the original story while he marked corrections.

Another series of steps followed. I'd already viewed the production process in journalism class films, with their sheets of newsprint moving to clanky sound tracks. But now I saw it first-hand. It involved making corrections, locking the frame ("putting the paper to bed"), and making a mold for the cylindrical presses. After the presses spewed out the news in print, came the cutting, assembling, and distribution of the weekly *Review*. Here was a newspaper that spread information, letters, and opinions about local, state, and national events, all over town – and beyond.

I didn't make the connection then, but now I see why Grandpa wanted to be published – to sell his point of view to an ever-wider audience, just as he ranged over the state to sell insurance for a livelihood. Nor did I realize I might be there because *Grandpa* loved to write, and wanted others to do so.

He was compelled to write. He was always writing books, pamphlets, and articles. He was always submitting manuscripts, which were often rejected.

> By the way, didn't I tell you last winter that I did contribute "Three Parsons" to the *Atlantic* Prize Contest? I rather think that I shall revise it this winter and resubmit it. I shall make a much better opening chapter, and try to break up my own wordiness into sunny openings.
>
> E. Dudley Parsons
> P.S. I do not yet admit frustration![40]

In an earlier letter, he had admonished Dad to write, as soon as Dad landed in India:

First, some personal experiences and observations on Indian life for the *Atlantic*; second, comment on the political situation for the *New Republic* or *Nation*; and third, some contributions of an educational type for *School & Society*, the *School Review* or the *Educational Review* or, for some chemical journal.

Strength to your pen, and mind![41]

He even encouraged Grandma to enroll in a writing class, which she reported in a letter:

The class that I have joined in magazine writing is proving invaluable. . . . Our articles are read in class if we so desire, or we read them ourselves, after which they are jumped upon by the class.[42]

And now I was in his sightline. He wanted me to move from journalism class to a working newspaper. I *did* enjoy *The Buzzette*, so it was easy to go along with his idea.

Each week, I sat at my desk typing items for the "Hopkins Notes." This was the town's social news, but "social news" didn't match me, with my round pink eyeglasses, limp brown hair, second-hand wardrobe, saddle shoes, and diffident personality. It was good that I could work using a telephone, for in-person interviews would have undermined any job-related authority.

When the black rotary phone on my desk rang, the caller informed me about events in Hopkins households, for items in what I thought of as "my column."

Mrs. Luther Nelson entertained four others for coffee on Wednesday morning at ten. She introduced Alma Smith, Grace Benson and Susan Youngdahl to her cousin Clara Nelson from Peoria, who is visiting for the week.

(I made this up, but it's close to what I wrote each week.)

Sometimes Mr. Markham told me to scare up news by contacting some of the "regulars" to learn about their visitors for coffee, their luncheon plans, or vacation trips to the Black Hills in South Dakota. Sometimes I described a wedding. I included the bride's dress and bouquet (stephanotis were popular), attendants' names, the church, and the families' hometowns. After several months, I began to recognize recurring names and activities in telephone reports: coffee gatherings, guests who played cards at each other's homes, out-of-town visitors, graduations, and vacation trips.

I could have used this experience to learn about the social fabric of a Minnesota town. But I was too naïve to learn from my grandfather. He saw fodder for his column in every chance encounter. A conversation about reading became instruction:

Reading Note

I called the attention of a fellow church member the other evening to a lone copy of the *New Republic* among the westerns, the movie periodicals, the astrological numbers and other "popular" issues. To my surprise, he said that he never had read one. And so, I gave a list of weeklies that discuss domestic and foreign affairs. Doing so, perhaps I may also serve some other inquirer:

The New Republic
The Nation
The Christian Century
Lafollette's Weekly
The Nation's Business[43]

A reader's letter provided a chance for banter:

A Reader Writes

Dear Morningsider -: Of late I have missed your verse. Not that I cared so much for it – but, you know, one gets used to things. How come?

Alden Grimes Crocker

Dear Mr. Crocker -: The drought dried up the spring of my enthusiasm. One look at my bleached corn, my jaundiced cucumbers, my shriveled potatoes, and my discouraged tomatoes, and I seem to want to retire within my study and rest my head on the bosom of Mother History. I "can't take it," as a versifier ought to be able to. But out of respect for you, Mr. Crocker, I offer this little bit:

"To The Tall Corn"
You grip the earth with a surer hold
As the rain clouds pass you by,
Oh, yours is a hero's tale untold
As you answer the children's cry . . . .

Far down in the depths of the Maya land,
You were grass of the commonest kind,
But you followed the skill of a planter's hand,
And you are now the fruit of a fertile mind . . . . [44]

Grandpa's openness and perspective came from more sophistication than I possessed, as a seventeen-year-old. So as high school was coming to an end, I became less and less interested in coffee parties and weddings. The social news bored me. Perhaps I felt "too sophisticated." The opposite was true: my failure to be curious indicated a lack of humility. Humility is the beginning of sophistication.

Mr. Markham probably saw me falter. He gave me one assignment that took me beyond the social news: a review of the Hopkins High School production of a Shakespeare play. I felt important as I sat in the auditorium on a Friday night, alert, pencil and paper on my lap, waiting for the curtain to open. The setting was ordinary: theatre-style seats in an inclined semi-circle, the draped velvet curtain rippling with back-stage movement. Parents, grandparents, aunts, uncles, and friends waited for a superb production. The performance itself is lost to me. But I recall writing and re-writing the review, and feeling pleased when it was published because few of my golden words had been cut.

By the time I held this job, Grandpa's own column had become less regular. Had I been meant to carry on a tradition? If my grandfather dreamed of a writing career for me, then those dreams didn't take hold. My review of the play was a bump in a two-year, flat-line career. With no clear sense of vocation, I wandered into the College of Education at the University of Minnesota. Mr. Markham transferred me to the advertising office located on Miracle Mile in St. Louis Park, where I hung on for another year, quoting prices for advertisements over the phone and stuffing envelopes. Then I resigned. Grandpa had died in 1952, one year after I entered the doors of *The Hennepin County Review*. I didn't have to explain to him my drifting away from a career he might have envisioned for me.

But it seems I've been writing all along: journals, sermons, newsletter articles, reports, and now pieces for my grandchildren. My grandfather's writing intertwines with my own, so my grandchildren might meet him, and perceive their heritage. It's even possible that Jessica will love to write. One evening when seven years old, she attended a reading of memoirs in which I participated. After returning home, she opened the computer and began her own: "When I was born, I spoke Russian…"

And so a mysterious melding of memory, loss and hope occurs as I reflect on my family and its traditions. I wonder which of our values and experiences, if any, will take root and blossom in my children's children.

CHAPTER 22

Bulgaria Today

———

"TEN THOUSAND! WE HAVE TEN thousand!" Grandpa burst through my grandparents' front door, his one intense blue eye fixed on a piece of paper. He shoved it into the air, and waved it around as he charged forward. His stiff leg caused his uneven gait over the beige carpet, past Grandma's chair, and toward the kitchen. I don't recall who else was in this picture, or why the family had gathered there. But I hold an image of someone's wordless, flat response, a turning away from him. Was that Dad? Grandma? Whoever it was might have felt uneasy about Grandpa's excitement. Or, Grandpa wasn't to be taken seriously.

Grandpa's "ten thousand" referred to the number of petitioners signed up for some political initiative. Was it Henry Wallace's campaign to get onto the ballot in 1948? Maybe it marked a new level of Grandpa's political activity. Until then, he'd chaired meetings, presented reports, and engaged with politicians at the Saturday Lunch Club. He subscribed to offbeat papers such as *The Catholic Worker* and *Bulgaria Today,* and wrote letters to newspapers. He gave speeches at high school commencements, published articles about statesmen, and described village events in his newspaper column. He cornered neighbors for political conversation. But he had never held public office.

Grandma died some time after that successful petition, and Grandpa joined us at 4437 Brookside Terrace.

After he returned from his European trip, he filed in one of the Minnesota primaries, to run for President of the United States. He was ineligible to hold office because he'd been born in England of English parents. He was not a "natural-born" citizen.

Naturally, filing and running was his new challenge! To me, it seemed as ordinary as my family's preference for camping in tents and cooking over campfires, instead of taking vacations in lakeside cabins with real beds and stoves. It was in line with our family tradition beginning with Grandpa's own father, Great-Grandfather Henry William Parsons – a Non-Conformist Congregational minister from England, a justice-oriented crusader among African-Americans in North Carolina.

Surrounded by liberal friends during graduate school, I inserted information about Grandpa's action into some of our political chatter. Friends reacted to this as a piece of interesting trivia, and we'd return to our frustration with Eisenhower. Then I became quiet about family history for another year or two. I wondered about him occasionally, but my questions remained in the background.

Years later, I began to ask, *How could Grandpa have done such a thing? Why would he want to run for an office he couldn't hold?* And when was it, anyway? Was it in 1948, or 1952? (Those were two years when Minnesota held primaries, before reverting to the caucus system for a lengthy period of time.) I began to suppose my imagination had created this memory. I started to think I'd manufactured it to explain why my family didn't talk about him.

One day, in browsing through a scrapbook of Grandpa's papers, I found a clipping from *The Minneapolis Sunday Tribune.*

Can't Win
E. Dudley Parsons, 75-year-old Minneapolitan who entered the Minnesota presidential primary last week, can't be president

because he was born in England. His filing was accepted conditionally, however, pending a ruling by the state attorney general whether Parsons can legally run for the office.[45]

The accompanying photo shows him solemn-faced, in a pinstriped suit, his tie knotted correctly, his hair parted cleanly, his reverent gaze directed at a piece of paper on a desk.

The clipping settles the date. Since Grandpa was seventy-five years old and born in November 1876, then he must have filed for the Primary by the deadline of February 15, 1952. The Attorney General disqualified him from running soon after he filed. It was less than a year after Grandma's death.

Even after I figured out those facts, Grandpa's motives remained a puzzle.

Forty-five years after his attempt, I began to look for bits of information. I called Margaret in Minneapolis, with news about my children, and slipped in a question: "What was *that* all about?"

"Some man came to the house and persuaded him to run." I could hear her breath whistling. I didn't expect that answer. I'd imagined it was his idea.

"But who was that?" I asked her.

"I don't know. He was from the DFL."

"The DFL?" *That's impossible.*

"Yes. The DFL." End of conversation. "Keep quiet about this unpleasantness," she might as well have said. I gave my goodbye, and hung up to wonder some more.

By DFL, Margaret meant the Democratic Farmer-Labor Party. Hubert Humphrey had helped broker it into existence in 1944. It was a coalition of conservative urbanites and liberal unionists and farmers, which gained a strong base for the Democrats. But Grandfather's views were more like those of the Socialist Norman Thomas, or of Henry Wallace, the Progressive Party candidate in

1948. (When the Communist Party USA endorsed Wallace, his candidacy became a political disaster.)

It's hard to imagine a DFL leader's inviting Grandpa to be a candidate, since he would have been seen as a liability. However, there'd been a party schism in 1948. Humphrey's conservative group, which backed Truman, was pitted against the pro-Wallace group. Perhaps a residue of this schism was present in 1952. Perhaps the field merely seemed wide open.

I called my sister in California to ask what she thought. "I just think he felt the birthplace issue would disappear if he kept going," she responded. I argued with her: "No, don't you think that some politicians wanted to show popular support for far-left views?" She was silent. This meant she didn't agree, but wouldn't discuss it, either.

Months later, I asked my question of Margaret again. "It was one of his pals from those political discussions." She meant the Saturday Lunch Club. She didn't describe the conversation to me, but I can see it: the percolator plugged in on the kitchen counter, coffee cups and a plate of cookies or coffee cake on the dining room table. The man seated opposite Grandpa, with wintery sun casting shadows on the snow outside and pouring through the bay window. Margaret would have been upstairs with my two youngest brothers, trying to keep them out of the way. I can believe she didn't know the subject of the conversation at the time.

The Saturday Lunch Club source makes sense. Many of the members active in Progressive politics also belonged to the DFL, so I understand Margaret's original statement. A strategic decision by "some politicians" also seems right, if the context was division within the DFL and if "some politicians" were Grandpa's "pals." It's possible they hoped Grandpa could *run* for office – even though he couldn't *hold* office – so that left-leaning views would receive more exposure. Minnesota statutes then in force permitted an individual to file by affidavit, with 100 signatures on a petition from each of the nine Congressional Districts then in place. Grandpa and "his pals" must have used those mechanics.[46]

Recently I saw a copy of an archived inventory in the Minnesota Secretary of State's Election Division.[47] And there he is! Grandpa is listed, along with Eisenhower and six other candidates, in the 1952 Presidential primary. Following that list, I saw another name: "1952. Progressive Party: U.S. Senator: Marian LeSueur." Marian LeSueur and my grandfather were contemporaries, both active in the Saturday Lunch Club. They had co-authored a 1952 pamphlet for the club about its connections with the liberal movement.

I've concluded that the idea of Grandpa's running for public office was hatched within a group of Saturday Lunch Club contemporaries. As Margaret had said, "It was one of his pals from those political discussions."

My grandfather had plenty of self-discipline when it came to his books, articles, speeches, garden, or in writing multiple letters to newspapers. He had a broad understanding of history and was a devoted observer of local, state, and national politics. But this idea of running for President? Did he latch on immediately? Did he give it any thought? Did he see himself as sacrifice for a cause? I'll never know.

Nor do I know how he told the family about his decision. It would be like him to announce it at suppertime, with my father looking at his plate, silent, planning to delay a response until he'd thought about it.

But at the time of my telephone exchange with Margaret, I told her, "You must have thought he was nuts."

Her swift response: "Yes, I did."

But *why* had my grandfather *responded* to "his pals?" That's my question. His powerful commitment to Progressive causes was always part of his make-up. I think he saw horizons but not stumbling blocks in the roads. He saw a society that eliminated inequities and provided social safety nets. But that horizon was receding. The Cold War and fear-driven association with Communism obscured it.

He had lost something else: his vital connection with Grandma, dead since June 1951. He wrote this lament on the flyleaf of his *Encyclopedia Britannica Atlas* (one of the odd places where he habitually scribbled notes):

> July 9 Why have I not written since April? Well there have been several reasons chief of which was the death of Clara who has lived with me as wife, mother, grandmother since our wedding-day in December of 1905.... As I watch the things she gathered thru the years disappearing one by one either by gift or sale, I could easily lose myself in unavailing sorrow. There was the chair wherein she sat evening after evening as I faced her in my chair – it has gone for a few dollars to someone I know not who will doubtless find a new use for it. But I do not need it to give me the picture of her as she labored on the piece quilt that goes to little Rolf's bed, complete in every particular by reason of her persistence thru the winter and spring until the day before she died.[48]

Grandma had shared his ideals; they both cared deeply about peace. At the same time, she had provided balance, grounding, and practicality. She'd been able to rein him in. Within our family, she stabilized his volatile personality. With Grandma dead, Grandpa's grief must have been a strong factor, compelling his response to his political "pals." Perhaps he thought, "Someone has to stand up for what's right." Possibly he thought, "Now's the time." Maybe he was impelled to "do something." People do respond to loss in that way.

Disqualified but not discouraged, Grandpa maintained his zealous political interests. He continued writing letters to suburban and city newspapers, no doubt similar to this earlier one in *The Daily Times*:

THE SOVIET SIDE OF THE QUESTION
To the Editor, Daily Times:
Nowhere has the Soviet side of the current controversy over Iran been given. The papers, save a very few, and the radio commentators, with the same exception, constantly "ride" the Soviet for "aggression." Certainly no one need accept the Russian position, but a decent appreciation of justice demands that it be presented.

In 1921, the Soviets by treaty renounced all the privileges that czarist Russia had obtained from Persia by duress . . . . Later, another Iranian government, thinking less of the peasants than of the good of their landlords, permitted British and American oil interests to exploit parts of Iran.

E. DUDLEY PARSONS[49]

Other letters likely affirmed some of the social changes in the Soviet Union. Some might have censured the worsened relations between the United States and the USSR. Perhaps they demanded facts rather than ideology.

I note, too, that my grandfather expressly stated he was not in favor of imitating the Russians here in the United States, as he states in response to another letter.

To the Editor of The Tribune
But what amazes me in Mr. Hauser's letter is his implication that . . . I am necessarily in favor of imitating the Russians. No more would I do so than I would imitate the English school system because I realize its advantages over our own, or imitate

the French marriage system for its many good points or imitate the Hindu caste system because it has several distinct virtues to recommend it.

No, we Americans have within the limits of our own constitution the answer to our own problems . . . .
E. DUDLEY PARSONS[50]

These letters were not always well received:

IS E. DUDLEY PARSONS A REAL PERSON?
To the Editor

Is "E. Dudley Parsons" a real person or is it the nom de plume of some crackpot who is always writing to the Open Forum (or the letter column of any other paper who will publish his crackpot ideas)?

-- O. SWANSON
Montrose, Minn.
Editor's Note: E. Dudley Parsons is real.
His ideas are his own.[51]

His outspoken comments increased household unease. We experienced consequences. In another phone call to Carol, I learned how she'd been bullied: "I was waiting at the school-bus stop, and it was one of those freezing twenty-below days when we had to cover our noses with scarves so we could breathe." I imagined her stamping her feet to keep warm as other students gathered. She continued, "Some kids pried up stones from the railroad bed and threw them at me. They taunted me: *Commie, Commie.*"

At about that same time, Margaret later told me, a student had beaten up my brother Dudley at school; teachers didn't intervene (Dudley doesn't remember this incident). *Did I escape this treatment?*

I don't know. I wasn't involved in any high school "crowd," although I did have two close friends, also on the fringe. I was so socially uncomfortable that I would have been an outsider in any case. Our family didn't talk about being harassed or excluded. I like to think if we had, then Grandpa would have comforted us, but I suppose he would have named harassment to be the consequence of "taking the right stand."

Because Dad was a school administrator with tenure, and had clout in the teachers' union, we had some security. But no one knew when cause for termination might be found. He had the same name as Grandpa, so he had to produce explanations. He often had to deny he was the author of those letters. Even I, in my adolescent self-absorption, was aware of accusations, black lists, and broken careers. Newspapers reported concern about Communist infiltration in America – anxiety increased when Senator Joseph McCarthy claimed in February 1950 that there were 205 known Communists in the State Department. Grandpa noted this in an Atlas jotting:

> Hysteria is arising as in and after World War One, for we who want peace in the world are accused of being communists when we demand that lying and misrepresentation of Russia and close allies must stop. Perhaps some of us will have died [unclear] before the wretched fiasco is over.[52]

Grandpa's problematic opinions did break through my moody preoccupations with the promises and threats of high school life in a wealthy suburb. "Another nasty phone call last week," Margaret told me one day after school. "I answered the phone and this woman just asked 'How many do you have in your family?' 'Eight,' I told her. 'Well, how would you like eight one-way tickets to Russia?' And then she hung up. Just like that. Didn't even bother to say who she was."

Another time, I got off the school bus, collected mail from the street-side mailbox, and took it inside. Margaret sorted through flyers, letters, and bills, then slapped *Bulgaria Today* down onto the dining table. Then she went back to the garden, her principal means of self-soothing. Neighbors didn't provide comfort – in at least one election in that wealthy suburb of thousands, there were only four votes for Democratic candidates. Margaret and Dad cast two of them.

Eventually Margaret ordered my brothers "when you come home from school, get the mail, and if *Bulgaria Today* has arrived, don't even bring it into the house. Put it into the barrel for burning trash, and set it on fire. Here are the matches." No one dropping by for coffee could see evidence of Grandpa's interests or supposed loyalties.

Bulgaria Today into the burning barrel: there's an image for family challenges! It can't have been easy for Dad to be the quiet, steady one in the family. It must have been hard for Margaret to handle a dying mother-in-law, three stepchildren, two little ones, and my grandfather's subsequent insertion into the nuclear family. It would have been difficult for Grandpa to lose his beloved anchor, his home, and his position as head of household. Dad didn't share feelings with us children. Margaret directed the burning of *Bulgaria Today* without discussion.

CHAPTER 23

Grandpa's Last Journey

———

IN THE FALL OF 1952, I began my daily commute to University of Minnesota. It was seven months after the Attorney General had disqualified Grandpa for running in the Minnesota Primary. While I, a freshman, was investing energy in figuring out the University environment, Grandpa was summoning his energy for concerns more demanding than Progressive politics. He had been diagnosed with pancreatic cancer in August, after hiding his symptoms for several months. On learning the hopeless prognosis, Dad pursued every lead about possible treatments, including writing to research institutions in the United States and Canada. Nothing could be done.

Grandpa lay on his bed in the new room, covered with a light blanket. He was too weak to interact. He could turn his head to see hydrangeas outside the window growing in the shade of the blue spruce. Glints of light bounced off Minnehaha Creek as the ducks circled, quacked, and dove near the cattails. The redwood-paneled fireplace to his right, built for him, was empty of kindling and logs. It wasn't cold enough to light fires.

Straight ahead he could see the bookshelves holding his own father's gift of Biblical stories, illustrated by Durer –stories that fed their ideals. There, too, were copies of his pamphlet about Grandma, written to assuage his grief. His *Heroes of the Northwest*, his other books, and the signed edition of Sinclair Lewis' *Arrowsmith* were within eyesight. As he lay there, he could see family traditions lined up in print.

He needed nourishment and painkillers, which Margaret administered. Since Margaret had been a Nurse's Aide, she knew how to give shots and care for bedridden patients. This wasn't easy. Managing the household, caring for the garden, feeding three stepchildren and two preschoolers was a burden. Hospice didn't exist then, and we couldn't afford extra help. (After Grandpa died, she asked to be paid for his care from his meager estate. She had resented or felt unrecognized for her contribution.) Dad worked long hours, Carol and Dudley were caught up in their own schools, and our two young brothers were kept quiet when possible.

I avoided my dying Grandpa. But one day, when it was already dark, I arrived home from the University. Margaret said, "You should go in and see your grandfather." I walked down three steps into the dim room, and over to his bed. I said his name. His one seeing eye wandered to my face. For years, I always visualized him in that way: with one living eye, and one blind, dead, whitened eye. I now understand that I sometimes saw an empty socket for the missing eye, and that he sometimes used a glass eye.

I didn't know how to be with my grandfather in his dying. I didn't know how to sit there beside him and hold his hand. I didn't know that you could read out loud, or talk to someone, and describe your day. I didn't know that personal contact is nourishment. Instead, I looked down at him, stayed for a moment, and left the room.

Grandpa was dying on the fringe of my life. Now this seems incredible, but University life was my preoccupation. Each day Dad dropped me off on his way to work, after a largely silent commute. Sometimes I stayed until after supper and always returned home via three different streetcars. That's how it was one night, soon after seeing my grandfather in his room, that I climbed the stairs to my own room, fell into bed, and went to sleep right away.

Something awakened me. There was a bustling sound downstairs. I didn't investigate. I rolled over. I returned to heavy sleep.

He was gone. He who loved to travel had taken his last journey through illness and past death itself, to join the endless stream of life and death. I learned this the next morning when Margaret announced the news in the kitchen: "Your grandfather died last night." (I don't recall any ensuing conversation.) It was September 16, 1952, three weeks after I began my freshman year.

I know there was a funeral. I know I was there, but what was it like? It's disappeared from recollection. Nor do I understand why I can't recall the service for Grandpa, who was so ebullient and influential. Were his books mentioned? That *The Government of Minnesota* had met a need in high school history classes? That *Heroes of the Northwest*, used in elementary schools, had described the lives of those, such as the Mayo brothers, who were heroic without violence? Was anything said about the lively newspaper columns revealing a love for local history, endless curiosity about other people, and passion about wellbeing for the poor? And what about organic gardening – was this assumed to be a cranky approach to gardening in the marvelous age of DDT?

Perhaps the minister's words were focused on Grandpa's activities as a churchman: a founding member of our church, writing down the by-laws, serving as deacon, offering to the preacher criticisms of each Sunday's sermon on the way out the sanctuary door, casting the only "no" vote during a decision to buy a guest book for church visitors.

Did our pastor tell the story about Grandpa's late arrival one Sunday morning? He shared it with me years later: "I was standing in place giving the call to worship, Janet, and the third pew where your grandfather always sat was full. He walked in during the first hymn when everyone was standing, pushed into his usual seat on the aisle, and when the hymn ended he sat down first. Everyone else had to move one seat over – I watched them adjust – and the last person was left standing, forced to find another pew."

I have seen a copy of the funeral service, which the minister had passed on to Dad. He had included Walter Rauschenbusch's version of II Corinthians 13, a Social Gospel paraphrase consistent with the melding of Grandpa's Christian and social convictions:

> Love is just and kind. Love is not greedy and covetous. Love exploits no one; it takes no unearned gain: it gives more than it gets. Love does not break down the lives of others to make wealth for itself; it makes wealth to build the life of all. Love seeks solidarity; it tolerates no divisions; it prefers equal workmates; it shares its efficiency. Love enriches all men, educates all men, gladdens all men . . . . [53]

I assume we gathered as a family afterward. After Grandma's funeral, the house had been filled with laughter; food was piled on the dining room table. But Grandpa's gathering is lost to me.

One obituary described his outlook:

> To thousands of daily newspaper readers of the Twin Cities the name E. Dudley Parsons is synonymous with "radical". He knew as much, but it did not deter him. He never faltered in the prosecution of his honest economic and political views. Nor could he ever be persuaded to "tone down" his views on these subjects. [54]

I've conducted many memorial services over the years, and know they open up abundant emotion. I wonder about the range of feelings that attended Grandpa's: anger about the fall-out from his politics, relief that he was gone, sadness over his loss, and regret about our inability to stop the disease. These must have been among our feelings. My own response came later: a fascination with his personality and a search for understanding.

At the time, I went into my default mode: numbness in response to loss. In an eight-year period I had lost my mother, grandmother, grandfather, and my Alden Drive home. I had entered the confusion of a new family constellation.

But my default mode also involves leaping into activity. University life was handy for that. There were studies. There were new friends, gained at the Congregational Student Center and through inter-religious events. There were long streetcar rides with a fellow student from high school days. There was my part-time job in the advertising office of *The Hennepin County Review* and *The St. Louis Park Dispatch*.

These activities loosened connections with my family and its traditions. Or so I thought.

Parsons Family, ca. 1942.
Back row, left to right: Luella Christine Austin Parsons, E. Dudley Parsons, Jr.
Front row, left to right: Carol Louise, Janet Roshanara, Ernest Dudley III

E. Dudley Parsons, Sr.

E. Dudley Parsons, Sr. and Clara Dickey Parsons, Summer 1944

Ernest Parsons, date unknown

1941
Front Row: Carol Parsons, Janet Parsons.
Middle Row: Margaret Anna Larson, Claus Larson (her father),
Clara Larson (her mother), Katherine Larson (her sister), Luella Austin
Parsons. (Clara Larson is Luella Parsons' first cousin.)
Back Row: extended family members
(Coleman Larson – Margaret's brother – is second from left).

Front: Clara Larson; Rear: Katherine Larson, Luella
Austin, Margaret Larson; date and place unknown

Can't Win E. Dudley Parsons, 75-year-old Minneapolitan who entered the Minnesota presidential primary last week, can't be president because he was born in England. His filing was accepted conditionally, however, pending a ruling by the state attorney general whether Parsons can legally run although ineligible for the office.

"Can't Win," *Minneapolis Sunday Tribune*, February 17, 1952.

Margaret Larson Parsons and E. Dudley Parsons, Jr. 1994

The Reverend Henry William Parsons, date unknown

CHAPTER 24

The Committee on the Russian Achievement

———

WHILE LEARNING ABOUT STUDENT LIFE at "the U," I continued to frequent the Congregational Student Center. It was a place to meet friends, eat my bagged lunch, and feel comfortable within a vast environment. One day, while heading for the refrigerator, I ran into a graduate student.

He'd been doing research in the Minnesota Historical Society, he explained, and had come across a "piece on Russia by your grandfather. It was well-researched." He spoke as though he had more to say. I felt he was appreciative, and accepted the support he seemed to offer. By this time, he might have known about Grandpa's death. He must have been aware that Grandpa had been a controversial figure.

I wonder how that student would evaluate the research today. It's a pamphlet titled "The Report of the Committee on the Russian Achievement." When I first saw it more than forty years after that conversation, I'd had my first trip to Russia and had read some Russian history. I was startled by its title. (This was the pamphlet I was to mistakenly name "On the Success of the Russian Experiment," at a meeting in Yaroslavl in 1998.)

It's small, with a note on the cover: "Private copy, CDP [Clara Dickey Parsons]." Grandma must have approved, to keep it so carefully. Grandpa was chairman of the committee, which printed and presented the report to the Saturday Lunch Club in 1936. It was he who had proposed the idea for the investigation. I imagine his saying, in response to statements about the USSR, "Let's see if these are true." The original chairman of the committee could not serve (or chose not to), so Grandpa was appointed. Or stepped forward. He might have edited the final version, too.

The response had been mixed:

Russia

In 1936, as chairman of a committee of the Saturday Lunch Club, I presented an objective report entitled, "The Russian Achievement." It was based on an examination of some thirty or more studies of various phases of the Russian "experiment" by approved scholars who had no axes to grind – politically, socially, economically or otherwise. One study, for instance, was made jointly by the commissioners of health of New York City and London; another (on family relations) by Dr. Mary Fairchild, of Bryn Mawr College. I was nearly torn in pieces by various members of that supposedly liberal club, and only in the last year have they begun to believe such conservative observers as Joseph Davies (Mission to Moscow), and Wendell Willkie. But now, even The Saturday Evening Post gives space to Edgar Snow's revealing notes on what goes on behind the Russian front. Am I happy?[55]

The report is well argued. It poses seven questions, such as "Is collective farming successful?" and "Who have suffered from the regime?" Each section summarizes the committee's response to the question and provides a bibliography.

As I look through this pamphlet, it's hard to separate the committee's presentation from my impression of their naïveté.

The report refers, for instance, to the 2,000-mile canal between the Baltic and White Seas. It describes the workers on this canal as adequately paid "redeemed criminals." This was put as a contrast to a punitive attitude toward criminals in America. (The Saturday Lunch Club had debated prison reform at one of its meetings.) But now we know that tens of thousands of slave laborers from the Gulag died while working in extreme conditions on this canal, which was never fully utilized. It was too shallow.

The report, I realized, was written during the Great Terror when Russians were shot, sent to the Gulag, or detained without trial. When presented, it was two or three years after the infamous show trials, which Walter Duranty of the *New York Times* had observed. Duranty was Moscow Bureau chief for the *Times* and had won the Pulitzer Prize in 1932. His regular dispatches to the paper became a source for "The Report of the Committee on the Russian Achievement." A local newspaper had published an article by Duranty, and Grandpa wrote to praise the editor:

Duranty Articles Praised

To the Editor: I desire to thank you for publishing the account of the Soviet economy and of social improvement by Walter Duranty. He is perhaps our very greatest reporter, as he keeps his opinions entirely out of his factual presentation . . . .
E. DUDLEY PARSONS[56]

Historians now discredit Duranty's reporting. He had observed the engineered famine in Ukraine, but betrayed his readers by naming it "a disappointing harvest." Duranty's association with the *Times* could have provided credibility for the Saturday Lunch Club liberals. Moreover, newspaper accounts of events occurring in the Soviet Union were confusing. Liberals couldn't believe the few reports of true conditions in the USSR, because they didn't fit into their view of Russians moving toward a dream world.

Grandpa died before Khrushchev's secret speech to the Twentieth Party Congress in 1956, which exposed Stalin's terror to Russian leaders. As far as I know, E. Dudley Parsons, Sr. never admitted to family members that there might have been something wrong in the Soviet Union. Given his stubbornness and love for good argument, I wonder: *how long would it have taken him to accept Khrushchev's disclosures?*

I don't know if Grandpa was ever open to questions about famine in Ukraine, repression in the USSR, or Stalin's dictatorship. Perhaps he was one of those who could not believe these conditions. Maybe he used these questions as foil to arguments for the good: the Metro system (built with forced labor), increased availability of education, medical care, and housing. He maintained his reputation as a radical until he died.

When Grandpa was alive, I wasn't aware of the extent of that reputation, but as stories accumulated my understanding expanded. Years after Grandpa's death, Aunt Peg told me how shocked she and Uncle Edgar had been when they arrived in Minnesota for their annual visit. "We stayed overnight in Wisconsin, got up early, and drove to Stillwater for breakfast. The waitress poured our coffee, we opened the newspaper and – you cannot imagine! You can*not* imagine! What it was *like*! To see that headline on the front page! 'Ten Known Communists in Minneapolis.' And E.D.'s name was on the list."

Our grandfather's reputation and our family's embarrassment must have seeped into my feelings about his vocal support of Russia. That's why the student's remark about a "well-researched paper" felt like support. Moreover, the "U" felt like a world of open discussion in a wide space, compared to my home's anxious constriction. University people were interested in books and ideas! But on Brookside Terrace we kept silent about Grandpa's views, and understood we were to dismiss his radical posture. I can't say how we knew this stricture. Neither Margaret nor Dad invited discussion, nor did we children ask questions in a family setting. If private exchanges occurred, then I wasn't involved. Nor were we told, "Don't talk about it." Our silence became a habit of barely conscious mutual consent. It was a family secret, something widely known but not discussed.

One day after my American Studies class concluded, and everyone was gathering up notebooks to head out the door, I heard my name. "Miss Parsons, can you stop for a minute?" The Professor and his assistant were standing next to the lectern at the front of the blackboard.

What's wrong? I get A's. I left my seat in the third row, moved past the wooden tablet-armed chairs, and arrived at the blackboard.

"Are you related to the E. Dudley Parsons who wrote letters to the newspapers?" They relaxed into delighted smiles when I said yes. This response surprised and pleased me. They didn't ask more questions, and I left for my next class, feeling that not everyone dismissed Grandpa.

I don't know whether or not my grandfather ever separated his own dream of ending income inequality from the USSR's devolution into Lenin's and Stalin's Communism. He wasn't alone in his inability to see the repression, slavery, and brutality. He might have used his bright, agile mind to bolster his passions rather than to scrutinize them. I understand that his insistent idealism made him look like a fringe character. He could be discounted. Yet his perspective was grounded in a knowledge and love of history, and a commitment to a better life for "have-nots." I see him an enthusiastic lover of ideas, a whole-hearted large-scale dreamer, a possibility personality.

Grandpa's wide reading contributed to his colorful writing. These assertions, written in a letter to my father in 1932, still resound with me:

I like your kick-back at my anti-imperialistic views (not anti-British), whether it is Spain murdering Atahualpa in Peru, or Montezuma's solders in Mexico, or Britain doing Hindus or Afghans or Chinese to death or the United States killing Indians in cold blood or raping the Philippines or showering bombs on the women and children of Nicaragua or cutting down the peasants of Haiti with machine-guns or Japan abusing Koreans or rampaging over Manchuria, one and the same cause stands horrid in the background – economic greed. It knows no justice nor no homeland; it smears blood over both the conquered and the conqueror and robs not only the "native" of his inheritance but the very minion of its power who slavishly follows its mandates. Witness the poor crippled, forsaken soldiers of the allies begging their way in a hundred cities or gasping out their lives in a hundred hospitals. At Fort Snelling alone are hundreds of decrepit shells of men who contribute daily of their number to the grave and scarcely anyone knows about it. And that is only one of many, many hospitals of the kind in America alone – and the war that took them forth to the poison that has been killing them ever since is only fourteen years away!"[57]

The first time I read those words in the nineteen-eighties, there was talk of bombing Nicaragua; now, who can avoid thinking about veterans of the Iraq and Afghanistan wars needing treatment in "many, many hospitals?" I recall, too, Russian men – veterans of the Russian-Afghan war – begging, without legs, on Moscow street corners, during my several travels in that city. My grandfather's views were not completely cuckoo – not to me, not now.

CHAPTER 25

Scraps

———

HERE'S A SURPRISE! A GREY-GREEN piece of cardboard proclaims Grandpa a 1912 delegate to the Hennepin County Republican Executive Committee.

I'm looking at an old scrapbook of Grandpa's "official papers," as Dad labeled it when he'd put the scrapbook together. It was like him – a way to order a puzzling life. A way to review his own origins, and ask *Where have I been, and how did I get here?* As I'm doing now. He did this for many family members. There's one for my mother. I have one, too, full of letters I'd written before I could afford long-distance phone calls. Some scrapbooks are small – life wasn't long. Some are unfinished – I'm still alive.

This one is full and complete, labeled *F. Dudley Parsons I* in Dad's block letters. First, a copy of Grandpa's birth registration, giving an address in Preston, England in 1876. After that, his citizenship certificate, gained when he was twenty-two. Then, several certificates inserted into sleeves that show, it seems to me, his finding his way as a teacher. Part-time pastoral work was interwoven with teaching. It looks as though he jumped around a lot, since there's a document for every year or two. Does this indicate a lack of focus, or an economic reality? But a thread does hold his life together: teaching certificates, and Home Missionary Society commissions. The commissions mean he was assigned to a small struggling congregation, or a church start up.

But how to account for this evidence of Republican affiliation? I form a supposition: by 1910, the Republican Party was in turmoil, with a Conservative wing, and a Progressive wing. Then Teddy Roosevelt left it, to form the Bull Moose Party for the 1912 election. Maybe Grandpa wanted in on the action. I don't know what he thought at the time, which policies he supported, whose views he endorsed. It seems that he became more radical as he aged, defying the adage that one begins youth as a radical, then ages into conservatism.

The book is packed with scraps, telling of books published, speeches given, articles written, loans taken out, money owed, letters of commendation, and notes for transacting business.

I turn over more leaves. In 1928 he retired from teaching at West High School to become a full-time insurance agent with Fidelity Mutual, where he'd worked part-time since 1920. But West High hadn't seen the last of him. I find copies of letters written in 1940, which incorporate earlier letters. An official had kept records. These reveal a long-running drama: a series of complaints about my grandfather's behavior.

The first complaints came while he was still on the faculty. In 1918, the Superintendent of Schools wrote Grandpa to say that the Board [of Education] will hold a hearing because "a question of loyalty on your part has been raised . . . ." It doesn't state the trigger for this question of loyalty; since there's nothing more about it, the hearing must have been held and concluded.

One L.S. Van Hook included this statement in a letter to the Assistant Superintendent of Schools, dated November 14, 1919:

Dear Sir:

I also want to call your attention to one E. Dudley Parson [sic], teacher at the West High School, who is not only a socialist, but is very radical; in fact it was because of the interference of his neighbors that he did not go down and put up a fight when you fired one of the professors a year ago, who was connected with the I.W.W. [International Workers of the World] movement. He is very strong on the class hatred. Says that capital is interfering with the proper running of schools, and many other things.

He is very desirous that the teachers organize and secure a charter and affiliate with the Federation of Labor . . . . [58]

At about the same time, the Public Examiner of financial records recorded an encounter (I can't name it a "conversation") about the manner in which Grandpa paid his lunchroom bills – once weekly rather than daily, as required. Grandpa claimed he'd never been told about the correct procedure ("that is a damn lie"). This was contrary to the lunchroom manager's testimony. Grandpa had also used her office to call *The Daily Star*, to assert that a recent Parent Teachers Meeting railroaded through a motion favoring military drill. The manager reported this incident to the Superintendent as a matter of disloyalty.

What is "disloyalty" in this context? Is it a failure to abide by the rules, and therefore a failure of loyalty to the school system? Or does it go beyond that, with freight from recent World War I atmosphere, which involved fear, suspicion, and need for loyalty to the country? Or was the first Red Scare doing its work? I don't know. Whatever principles were violated, Grandpa's behavior was provocative and disruptive.

I can't find the evidence behind another letter. In June 1923, an unidentified Assistant Superintendent wrote:

My dear Mr. Parsons:

I have gone carefully over the late unpleasantness with Mr. Boardman and Mr. McWhorter. I shall recommend you for reappointment.

I say to you distinctly now that I should not feel like tolerating another <u>outbreak</u> <u>of</u> <u>temper</u> <u>and</u> <u>bad</u> <u>manners</u> at the West High School; and I feel very sure that it would be quite difficult for me to place you in any other school of the city. I hope that no necessity for a transfer may arise . . . . [59]

The complaints mount. A high school student's parent spoke to the principal about Grandpa's provocative statements. The principal addressed a letter, dated April 3, 1925, to the Superintendent of Schools:

My dear Mr. Webster:
    This morning at 9:15 o'clock Mrs. L.W. Burgess, the mother of Marcia Burgess, an honor student in West High, appeared before me and . . . stated that in regular class work Mr. Parsons had made the following statements: "Lincoln was an accident and indecent." "Religion is all bosh." "Our Republic is all wrong." "LaFollette is entirely right." He discusses social subjects in no connection with the lesson. There is much more disorder in his classes than in other classes.
    . . . I have informed Mr. Parsons of these charges. he [sic] denies the statements, and says that they are wrongly interpreted. The matter is respectfully referred to you for your information and action. If what she says is true I recommend his dismissal from West High School.[60]

What was going on? Had he intended to spark discussion and debate? I know he didn't believe that "religion is all bosh." Did he think his high school English class would enjoy debate in the manner of the Saturday Lunch Club? Whatever his reason, his strong convictions weakened his internal stop sign.

It gets worse. Letters disclose that while selling insurance part-time, he entered the high school office to make and receive phone calls for his business. I can see him barging in, going behind the counter, and picking up the phone without asking. He used his students to get access to their homes in order to sell policies. And this behavior continued after he left teaching. A letter dated 1940 records Grandpa's treating the high school office as his own, during summertime, to call prospective customers. When asked to stop, he would pause, and begin again. The Principal ejected him from the building.

Information becomes more damning. An April letter describes another event:

To Whom It May Concern:

As I was correcting papers in my room at West High one evening after school, Mr. Parsons suddenly entered my room and commenced talking immediately about Finland and stated that Finland had antagonized Russia by building the Mannerheim line and that the conflict with Russia was entirely the fault of Finland – and much more to the same effect.

Knowing Mr. Parsons and realizing the futility of argument . . . I put on my wrap and went on toward the office. As I did so, <u>Mr. Parsons reminded me that he was still in the insurance business and urged me to consider taking some insurance with him just as he has done from time to time for</u> many years. . . . .

Mr. Parsons can hardly hope to gain sympathy at West High with his appeal for the Russian dictatorship, and his rather violent manner . . . may well have justified our principal in forcing him to leave.

(Signed) Ruth H. Hill[61]

I doubt that Grandpa shared that experience with Grandma, and of course it never came up during our well-mannered dinner-time conversations. Certainly these papers reveal a man impetuous in the service of his beliefs. His convictions did belong to an ongoing public debate about the best system to order our government. But where was his left brain during those instances?

The same tone shows up in some of his letters to editors, although he doesn't use "lies," or other pejorative language. But it's not there in his newspaper columns, speeches, or articles. In those, he could be folksy, inspiring, and thoughtful.

I wonder how many other scraps Grandpa got into. I wonder how to understand this unthinking side of my grandfather. Perhaps it arose from a deep uncertainty about money: *I have to bring in some income or else.* He'd grown up in the poverty of a rural clergy family, often paid in potatoes or a chicken. He was always chasing extra income. The family needed the small profits from houses my grandmother built. They had not been able to pay taxes on their Wisconsin properties. Their finances were Depression Era scraping by. If living on the edge reinforced his sense of poverty and inner fragility, then he responded with a scrappy spirit – sometimes useful, sometimes inconsiderate, usually lacking awareness of the consequences.

But it must have been more complex than that, more multifaceted than his ever-present concern about income. Grandma, although a loyal spouse, saw him clearly, as a letter to my father attests:

The effect of living with a restless spirit is not the easiest way to live. Your father has never lived in the present and enjoyed life to the fullest, I don't think. He is ever amidst the ruins of Pompeii or Egypt or wishing and longing to be going somewhere. I have never found anything that really made him contented. I remember when he was writing his first book and I was copying it long hand. I thought he would be quite peaceful for a while. He wasn't. . . . . He reads and during the process he gets so excited that he mutters to himself about the contents of the book. He walks down the street and he is mad at someone for not trimming his tree or cleaning his drive. It seems to me that a philosophy of life which never relaxes or accepts other's attitudes is most unsatisfactory. A philosophy of life which starts with itself and never gets away is quite wrong, I think. [62]

He couldn't recognize his impact on others. He was blind to it.

CHAPTER 26
Church

———

IT'S LOGICAL TO CONCLUDE THAT because Grandpa's church leadership intrigued me, I became an ordained pastor and embraced this family tradition. It's true that once I started to practice ministry, I understood how much he *had* influenced me. From the first, he insisted on introducing me to older church members, who treated me as a real person with contributions to make: "Janet, this is Waldo, who…" "You must meet Marjorie…" He conveyed that good things happen when church members meet and talk. I incorporated his approach later, when designing church learning experiences.

But I hadn't aspired to be a pastor. I assumed that women didn't become ministers, even though our denomination had ordained a woman as early as 1837. Our existing women pastors served small rural churches, mostly in northern small town New England; I didn't know any while growing up. I never saw an ordained woman until I was in college, and she didn't preach.

Yet, church life had been formative. At my grandparents' home, we knew we'd attend worship every Sunday, go to Sunday School, and participate in numerous activities. Among these were Quarterly Meetings. These were forums for deciding matters such as budget, building repairs, Sunday School curriculum, the calling of a new minister, or the need for a newsletter. Grandpa believed that the Holy Spirit worked through church members making decisions together, just as our tradition claimed.

When a meeting was due, he sprang into action to ensure a good turnout. He sat on a chair in the dining room corner, next to the table holding the black rotary phone. The shelf underneath housed a telephone book, a note pad, and a pencil tied to the table leg, to prevent Grandpa's walking away with it. Sometimes he called early or late, in his pajamas and robe, white chest hair sprouting above the collar.

"Are you coming to the church meeting?" His get-out-the-vote calls were abrupt, and sometimes without greeting. "It's important. We need a good showing." He'd hear the response, perhaps challenge it, and hang up without pleasantries.

In one meeting, I sat with him in the last row of chairs arranged in semi-circles. I was the only young person in a room full of grown-ups. Grandpa no doubt wanted me to learn "churchmanship," meaning "responsible membership."

The discussion was about purchasing a guest book.

This meeting might have been at the beginning of the post WWII population spurt, when churches grew so fast that leaders could neither analyze nor meet demands. That's probably why our minister introduced such a daring idea. With so many newcomers, a guest book could be a means for remembering names for follow-up calls on visitors.

Grandpa thought it a bad idea.

His view was: *In a real church, people are aware of newcomers.* They introduce themselves, are personally hospitable, take visitors to meet the pastor, give a tour of the church, and invite them to have coffee. He had a point. In a vibrant church community, members do extend warm welcome. When I became a pastor, however, it was difficult to remember unfamiliar names, or which person shared which concerns, while shaking hands after the benediction. I needed a guest book to bolster my memory.

The meeting discussion was lively, though short. Participants listened to Grandpa but backed the minister. When the voice vote was taken, Grandpa's was the only "no."

There wasn't rancor about that defeat. He must have known other causes when his opinion didn't prevail. He loved to participate in discussions, and when matters were decided he was ready to leap to the next issue. After all, he was the son of a Congregational minister. He had witnessed difference of opinion, drawn-out discussion, and unpopular decisions all his life.

Besides quarterly gatherings, activities included the church fair when Grandma dressed up like a gypsy woman. There were Christmas pageants, when the Three Wise Men wore exotic clothing, which Dad had brought home from India and the Middle East: shoes with curved tips, turbans, brocade coats, loose shirts cinched with bright sashes, and fez hats. One by one, Gaspar, Melchior and Balthazar walked down the center aisle toward the manger, wearing these items in several combinations, each singing a verse from "We Three Kings of Orient Are."

When I was in high school, a church leader called me just before the holidays. Her voice became hushed, indicating this call's importance. Would I play Mary in the Christmas pageant? All I had to do was sit behind the manger with downcast eyes. So I did, wearing a blue headscarf shading my pink-framed eyeglasses. As Balthazar approached, singing, "Myrrh is mine, its bitter perfume . . ." I gazed reverently at the manger's occupant: a glowing light bulb, representing baby Jesus, the Light of the World.

Church members produced plays in the social hall, which featured a stage, footlights, and a sound system. When I was in high school, the youth group performed a number of skits and short plays. I acted in two of these and can't forget that, in the second play, I didn't know my lines. My grandparents and Dad had kept asking me "Janet, have you practiced your lines?" I always assured them I had. This was a lie. I intended to master them later in the evening or the next day. I did give them several once-overs, but when opening night arrived, I wasn't aware I was in trouble.

But there I was, foundering, early in Act I, Scene II. I thought I was carrying on, but I'd grabbed lines from Act III and inserted them into the dialogue. When I became aware of the prompter hissing at me from behind the curtain, I was powerless and desperate. It was too late. The snatched lines gave away the denouement, leaving actors and audience confused. We went home in silence.

My grandparents were key members in starting Edina-Morningside Church, but it wasn't the only one in which Grandpa was active. There were at least five others, including New Brighton, Minnesota, where he and his father had served together. Although he wasn't ordained, Grandpa was licensed, which meant he could function as a short-term pastor in churches lacking a "settled" minister. Or he could preach for a minister on sick leave, or for one taking a vacation. He did this for years, both in Minnesota and Wisconsin.

One summer Sunday, I boarded a bus with him to head to a town in Wisconsin. I sat in the pew as he conducted worship. It was like many rural or small town sanctuaries: dark wood in the interior, a musty smell, stained glass windows with geometric designs, a pulpit in the center of the raised chancel, and a communion table on the floor centered under the pulpit. Perhaps a piano accompanied our hymns, rather than an organ. I wonder what his sermon was about. Was it the passage from the Book of Acts, which described the common life of early Christians, when no one had need? It's a passage I always associate with my grandfather, instead of the Apostle Peter: "Now the whole group of those who believed were of one heart and soul, and no one claimed private ownership of any possessions, but everything they owned was held in common . . . . There was not a needy person among them . . . ."[63]

Long after Grandpa died, but when the McCarthy Era was still fresh, I came across a letter from the Superintendent of Congregational Churches in Wisconsin. It informed Grandpa that his license to preach had been revoked. It didn't state the reason, but I knew it was because his political opinions had spilled into his sermons. He didn't distinguish between the Christian faith and fair income distribution. In Congregational governance the Superintendent's action would have called for a personal meeting with Grandpa. The decision must have stung him. It upset me, as I held that piece of paper, rereading the letter. It was another reminder that my grandfather's stating his convictions brought unpleasant consequences. I wish I could see it again, but it must have been discarded.

I sometimes wonder about my own caution in expressing strong opinions from the pulpit. It's true that a pastor must not violate tax law by using the pulpit to back a political party, candidate, or platform. But there are other factors, too. My personality? My interest in the context of Biblical stories? My desire to be fair and kind to all those sitting in the pews? I wonder if I fear consequences, even though my fear might not be well grounded. My caution is likely a mixture of all these factors; I don't think I'll ever know.

Grandpa did all he could to nurture my church participation, but it was Grandma who showed me that women could be church leaders. She had been the Church School Superintendent, and I knew she'd been the organist during the church's beginnings. These were acceptable – and important – roles for women at the time. However, she planted a different seed during a dinnertime story.

She was talking about their drive to Texas, where Uncle Edgar and Aunt Peg were to be married. "We stayed overnight in Oklahoma and left early to start driving again. It was a Sunday. We drove through more than one town, but couldn't find a church." She probably meant a progressive church like ours. An appropriate church. "It was getting late, so we pulled off the road, sat under a tree, and had lunch. I preached the sermon."

I took in Grandma's statement. I was alert to it. A woman and a sermon could go together. This was new information. I stored it away for thirty-four years. It wasn't until the nineteen seventies that I summoned courage to become ordained. I was freed when I saw I'd live beyond my own forty-fourth birthday – my mother's age when she had died.

Today, after having practiced ministry for forty-seven years (thirty-three of them ordained), I'm still fascinated by the lively community of the church. I love to see how members disagree, work together, change procedures, start something new, find ways to address need. (But I never try to memorize a sermon – the memory of that high school play sticks with me.)

I love the rhythm of the church year; its cycles of readings are life-markers. Advent, Christmas, and Epiphany, then Lent, Easter, Pentecost, and Ordinary Time move me through the seasons. I love the recurring Biblical passages, providing themes and stories to be examined in ever changing light, in differing contexts, and with new questions. Church was different for Grandpa and Grandma, yet it feels as though I continue to meet them in its life. It's a place where they come alive. In our tradition, it's called the Communion of Saints.

CHAPTER 27

Interrogation

———

IN SPITE OF THE NINETEEN-FIFTIES Red Scare and our family's silence about Grandpa's political views, his personality and passions keep on surfacing. It's as though he shoves his way into our company and we have to change our seats. It's like being one of the churchgoers who adjusted in their pews that Sunday when Grandpa showed up late for the Sunday service. During one of my phone conversations with Margaret about Grandpa's filing in the 1952 primary, she told me that in the late fifties, Coast Guard officers had interrogated my brother, E. Dudley the Third. He was too young while Grandpa was alive to know very much about Grandpa's ideals. I needed to talk with my brother about this. I had wanted to broach the subject for a long time, so when I was in Minnesota during a visit in 2005, I had my chance.

We stopped for lunch while on an excursion to look for eagles along the Mississippi River. The hostess seated us at a corner table in the dim dining room of an old inn. It's the kind of inn found in Minnesota river-towns: wood panels, patterned curtains (cream, orange, brown), and small lamps with perky shades.

"I seem to recall that you were interrogated by the Coast Guard? But I don't think you told me about it at the time. What was that all about?" I launched into the question after we recalled his visit to me in New Haven, in the late nineteen-fifties. He was then stationed at the Base in Groton, Connecticut.

He put his roast beef sandwich down on the plate, took up his fork, put that back next to his salad, and slumped forward to stare at the table.

"It was traumatic. I hadn't been there that long, and my Unit Commander called me in and said 'The Base Commander wants to see you. Report to him at 0800.'

"So the next morning I reported to the Base Commander at 0800, and the Base Commander said 'Coast Guard Intelligence wants to speak with you.' And two officers came in."

Right away they began to hammer him with questions: "What do you know about your father's activities in the Communist Party? What do you know about your mother's activities in the Communist Party?" The officers kept after my brother with question after question. He was completely confused and answered, time after time, that he didn't know.

He picked up his fork again, ate a shard of tomato, and gulped some beer along with a piece of sandwich. He looked too upset to enjoy his food. I began to feel sorry about bringing up the matter, but not sorry enough to stop. I wanted to know.

"Then they showed me a list of nine Communist organizations he belonged to," he said.

"My God. How awful."

"It was horrible." The Intelligence Officers let him go for lunch. He was in tears. "Not during the questioning," he was quick to add, "but all during lunch." He decided to call Margaret, who reminded him that Dad had received secret clearance after Grandpa died. My brother had known this, but was too flustered and upset to put it all together. After lunch he gave the officers that information.

"They had totally confused Dad and Grandpa," he continued. "Well, we all have the same name, and they both graduated from Hamline University."

"Wait a minute. They showed you a list of *nine* Communist organizations?" Now it was my turn to stop eating.

"Nine that Grandpa belonged to." *I'd never heard this one before.* I planted my elbows on the table and stared at him.

"They *said* he belonged to."

"Well, no. He belonged."

"But Grandpa wasn't a Communist! He was a committed Progressive, but never a Communist. I came across one of his *Atlas* journal entries from 1950 that said something like "There is increased tension everywhere. Some of us are being called Communists when all we want is peace." I carried on about our grandparents' Progressive and Socialist friends, their love of political activities, political conversation, political debate, and the widespread interest in the best way to run an economy.

My brother countered "Well, yes, but those groups were infiltrated, and considered Communist front organizations. I always knew he was a little funny." He lifted his palm and wagged it from side to side.

I didn't agree that Grandpa was "funny," but kept silent.

"And Grandma was a member of the Women's International League for Peace and Freedom," he added. I knew the organization – founded in 1915 with Jane Addams as its first president – had been considered suspect during the McCarthy Era.

I feel proud that my grandparents held onto their ideals, even during the hysteria and blacklisting that developed after World War II. I wonder if they were surprised and confused by the growing political tensions over what must have seemed to them to be a sensible way to equalize the world's resources. I don't know if they ever positioned themselves in any one place on a political continuum of Liberal-Progressive-Socialist, although I'm sure they always voted Democratic. Dudley was right, however, about some of the organizations that Grandpa joined. I have a copy of a letter, which identifies him as a member of the Minneapolis Chapter, American Peace Crusade. This letter further states that he was to be a delegate to the national meeting in Washington, D.C. in April

1952. Certainly this organization had been suspect, and probably infiltrated.

Although I was surprised that my brother, half a century after the interrogation, was still so affected by it, I was glad to see him begin to relax. He picked up his sandwich again and resumed eating. I wanted to know the outcome. "So then what happened? Did anyone ever apologize to you?"

"No. Not really. After they asked me more questions, one of them finally left and came back after awhile, and admitted they'd made a mistake. It was horrible."

He had been only eighteen. It was 1957 and his first extended stay away from home. My stomach feels unsettled whenever I think about his age at the time. Margaret had told me once that one of Dudley's teachers had made a demeaning statement to him, and I wanted to know more, but I set that question aside. I didn't want to be the interrogator any longer. We made our plans to visit the Eagle Center and the return drive along the Mississippi. Then we settled the bill and went out into the daylight.

CHAPTER 28
My Socialist Experiment

———

IT WAS A SUNNY DAY in June 1960. I was carrying a picket sign in front of the New Haven Connecticut Woolworth's. Several of us were walking in a circle on the sidewalk, holding signs demanding a boycott of the five-and-dime chain. Perhaps my grandfather's ghost was there, cheering me on. But where he was vocal in his stance for equal rights, I was struggling with my introverted self. Carrying a picket sign was a stretch.

Earlier that year, four African-American college students had ordered food at a lunch counter in a North Carolina Woolworth's. The manager refused to serve them, maintaining a "whites-only" policy. The students "sat-in," leading to further sit-ins, multiple news stories, a growing number of supporters, and an NAACP boycott. Because the New Haven store managers did employ and serve African-Americans, they couldn't have been pleased about our actions. But the NAACP organizers thought that publicity and economic pressure could change policy throughout the chain.

I arrived at the demonstration shortly after beginning work in a housing project. With a new degree from Yale Divinity School in hand, I had joined a Group Ministry – seven of us committed to living in the housing project and its neighborhood. We received salaries on the same level as the residents' incomes. We didn't want to be do-gooders driving in from suburbs.

Occasional foundation grants and church gifts funded our organization, but resources were thin. The staff car – a blue GMC Carryall – was a wreck. For a while, anyone who drove it in the rain needed a passenger. This person's job was to work the windshield wipers through open windows, using strings to pull the wipers back and forth. It made for a damp, sight-impaired ride. When I used the GMC, I began the workday – in my high heels – by opening the hood, punching open an oilcan with a mechanic's spout, and emptying it into the engine's thirsty receptacle. Then I could start the engine. The gas gauge didn't work, and I hated it when I ran out of fuel because I had forgotten to note the mileage at the previous fill-up.

One night at the end of a month the phone rang. It was my colleague: "Do you have any food?"

"Two eggs and some coffee."

"I have two eggs and some onions. If we ate together we could make a meal."

Agreed!

Over our omelets, I learned that the group's bank account was nearly empty. Payday was the next day. Staff members had urged the senior minister to work on stabilizing income. We needed more grant money or larger (and regular) church donations. We needed a cushion. We wanted him to focus on raising the bucks, but his response was "God will provide." On the day after our omelets, a check for $2000 arrived in the office. I was glad to be paid, but irritated. I wanted our leader to hear us say: "We hate this anxiety!" I wanted to hear *him* say, "I'm changing my strategy. I'm making a plan."

Staff members divided the group's income according to needs. Each November, we presented personal budgets and jointly determined our lean salaries. Though single, I received more than a family of three with independent assets. This seemed natural, normal and right, for we aspired to be like the early church as described in the Book of Acts:

> Now the whole group of those who believed were of one heart and soul, and no one claimed private ownership of any possessions, but everything they owned was held in common.... There was not a needy person among them, for as many as owned lands or houses sold them and brought the proceeds of what was sold. They laid it at the apostles' feet and it was distributed to each as any had need.[64]

I believed in our programs, the people I met, and our causes. We provided activities for children. We gathered adults in weekly meetings to hear concerns about their children, their jobs, and their safety. We drove women across the border to New York to obtain contraceptives, which were illegal in Connecticut at the time. We distributed leaflets to urge Fair Housing laws. We participated in the March on Washington. For five years, I worked hard within this version of progressive Christianity.

Now I think I was trying out my grandfather's political legacy. He would have been thrilled. A radical Christian tradition permeated his own thinking, coming from his father, whose preaching was rooted in Non-Conformist English Christianity. It came from Grandpa's reading of the Biblical prophets, who condemned exploitation. It came from his fascination with Russian history and its Revolution. Those stories about family ideals have a way of surfacing. Perhaps these stories *needed* to come to life again – even on the sidewalk in front of Woolworth's, where I see myself walking the picket line, taking my turn to explain our motives to passers-by.

Other picketers were engaging in dialogue; my approach involved commanding: "Lady, don't go in there! Stop! They won't desegregate Woolworth's in the South!" This method didn't change attitudes.

A woman approached me. She wore navy pumps, a navy suit with a white blouse, and a navy hat, which set off her curly white hair. *Maybe she wants to ask about the boycott.* She moved closer. Closer. She sent a spray of spit into my face. I stepped back, startled and angry. She continued to walk past.

In the housing project, I had met strong men and women who loved their children, made a life, and endured. But I didn't endure – a radical life demands a long hard slog. I couldn't accept being spit on while working for a cause. That was only the first of a series of challenges and irritations. Scraping by got old. I tired of so many omelets for dinner, hand-propelled windshield wipers, and broken gas gauges. I got sick of sweeping up plaster when it dribbled off my apartment walls. When I made presentations at suburban churches, I envied the women's clothing and longed for a decent haircut. I subscribed to *The Catholic Worker* (twenty-five cents per year), just as my grandparents had done. But I never saw myself as a Protestant version of Dorothy Day, the saintly woman who lived on the Lower East Side, shared life with welfare recipients, and ate in the soup kitchen at the Catholic Workers' House.

I know I received more than I gave: a view of strength within a crushing environment. I won't forget Mattie (twenty-five years old, as I was) who fed five children nutritious meals on a low income. Nor Hank, hit on the head by a teenager's hurled bottle. Hank's response was to form a basketball team. There was Art, who overcame heroin addiction, and the African-American pastors who dared challenge the police's treatment of a prostitute, in a time heavy with racial bias.

At the end of five years, I left the radical Christian group. I gave up the long slog for marriage, a suburban neighborhood, and eventually a solid career as a pastor. My horizon became closer, my focus sharper, my world smaller than that which my grandfather had dreamed about. Not worse. Just smaller.

Russia

CHAPTER 29

Surfacing in Russia

———

Dear Mom and Dad, not too much to report – it looks like I'll be coming home soon. I'm going to travel to Germany with Tom on the way back. We'll stay in cheap places – don't worry. By the way I found a job for next year. I met this Russian at a party and he's looking for English teachers, so I signed a contract to teach in Ulyanovsk. I'll be paid $25 a month, but don't worry I'll live on the Russian economy. More later, love, Steve.

MY YOUNGER SON STEVEN SENT this fax in the spring of 1993 while studying at Moscow State University. Between Grandpa's death in 1952 and that message, I had gained advanced degrees, worked, married, borne two children, and seen years fall away.

During my five years working in New Haven within that modified socialistic cell, I hadn't predicted that I'd visit Russia eleven times. It didn't occur to me that my younger son would work in Russia, marry there, and be the father of two bi-lingual children with dual citizenship. Never did I imagine myself pausing in front of an icon, exploring parts of old Moscow, traveling to Yaroslavl for a conversation with Russian women, walking my grandson to his preschool, or spending time in Russian Art Museums. Russia – the Soviet Union – the "gray country" – wasn't in the forefront of my interest during my New Haven life. Hearing the Yale Russian

187

Chorus, singing "Moscow Nights" at parties, or listening to Bill Coffin (the Chaplain at Yale) preach about peace and his trips to the Soviet Union – these had comprised the extent of my conscious curiosity about Russia.

Steven's interest in Russia began in high school. "I'm going to study Russian," he said one day. He was surveying the refrigerator's contents after school. "Oh," I responded, pleased but not puzzled. "Russian! What a good idea!" His decision had coincided with reading Dostoevsky and with writing a paper on Glasnost and Perestroika for an International Relations course. I encouraged Russian studies, even though a different language might have made more sense. *Why not Spanish? More employment opportunities! Hispanic immigrants are on the increase!*

I'm grateful for his choice. It's stretched me. His studying there, then his nearly ten years' living in Russia propelled me into reading about Russian history, culture, and politics. I began to see daily life in Russia through my own eyes, and those of my expanding family. My perception separated from my grandfather's powerful beliefs that in Russia, economic equality was being realized.

During Steven's semester in Moscow, my visiting him seemed impossible. His father went, but I was working in a conflicted church and the timing was poor. We couldn't talk with him on the phone. The dorm, which boasted feral cats roaming the building, was empty of functioning telephones. So we communicated by fax. Forty-five minutes on the Metro took him to the Central Telegraph Office each week. He read a fax from home and replied immediately, unless the system broke down. Some of those faxes are imprinted in my brain, word for word.

His first communications from Moscow State University seemed like previous laconic messages from the University of Wisconsin: he was right in the first place that he hadn't needed boots, because "the weather wasn't *that* cold." The food wasn't very good. After a while, Russian flavor began to appear: he had met someone named Katya. His group went to a performance of "Boris Godunov" (long, hard to understand, boring).

In one fax, Steven reported going to a dance in Lubyanka, the KGB building once graced by the statue of Felix Dzerzhinsky, Stalin's notorious KGB chief. A large basement room was crowded with a liberated rock band, many young men with buzz haircuts, and a few American students flickering in the strobe lights. I imagine that room to be near the corridor leading to the courtyard where prisoners were shot without trial during The Great Terror.

When Steven's message arrived, I called Dad, described the dance in the KGB building, and asked, "What do you think your father would say about that?" With an elegant – perhaps deliberate – misunderstanding he responded, "We-e-ll, he could be incredibly conservative, but I think he would have accepted dancing by *now*."

Then came notice announcing Steven's employment. Of course I'd encouraged both sons to study abroad for enrichment. But I had not meant $25 a month in Ulyanovsk. I responded:

> Steven! Are you frigging out of your mind? Did you abandon your cerebral cortex? Why did you go to college if not to practice thinking?

I didn't write that, but it describes my feelings. I tried again:

> Dear Son, I thought I was a better mother than this. What did I do to deserve such a thoughtless child? Didn't you know we'd worry about you constantly?

That guilt trip went into the wastebasket. This was the final result:

Dear Steven, we got your fax, and it looks as though you're committed to returning to Russia. Good for you! There's nothing like learning about another culture in a deep way. I looked up Ulyanovsk in the Atlas, and I see that it's on the other side of the Volga near the Urals. It's Lenin's birthplace, isn't it? Just a few questions – you've probably thought of these already. (1) Is there an American Consulate in Ulyanovsk? (2) What is your escape plan in case the present political situation gets worse? Will you be able to get to the Baltics or Finland without going through Moscow? (3) Is there a European Medical Center in Ulyanovsk, as in Moscow? (4) Will you have to pay for paper, pencils and books for your students? I read somewhere that teachers have to do this. Let us know your thoughts! Love you lots, Mom

After this, he sent several ordinary faxes about friends, teachers, the dorm, and bad food. At last, relief came in the form of a buried sentence: "Oh by the way at a party I was talking to this girl and she said I'd hate it in Ulyanovsk so I broke the contract."

Steven returned home in late May and made plans to return to Russia in the fall of 1993. "I'll go on a tourist visa, find work, and get a new visa. I met Americans over there who did that. You can get work as a guard at the Embassy – they'll help you change your visa." (He was wrong. Regulations don't permit this.) "You can't stop me." He was anticipating active resistance.

He removed all his savings from the bank – money I'd forced him to set aside with the promise, "This money can be for something big that you'll want some day." I was conflicted. I wanted to support his dreams, but Russia was far away and in political turmoil. It felt dangerous.

I called Dad. "Steven wants to live in Russia for a year, but it's so far away."

"Well," he said – I suppose to reassure me – "I went to India and ended up staying for six years. Your grandmother adjusted, and we returned home."

Six years! I didn't want to hear that. I decided that if Steven wanted to go badly enough, he'd have to handle arrangements without my help. He did. He persuaded Tom, a college friend, to join him. He obtained his tourist visa, and bought his airline ticket.

The situation was dire. In August 1991, there had been an attempted coup against Gorbachev. Yeltsin was now in power, and news reports described more unrest: hard-liners occupied the Parliament building known as the Russian White House. Ordinary people were dealing with hyperinflation, and breadlines were back.

I drove him to the airport and stood in line with him. I wanted to reach over and tear up his visa. It was October 2, 1993, and we said goodbye with mutual hugs and my forced blessing. I drove home carefully. I tried to lower my anxiety. I made dinner like a robot. I began to prepare for the next day's work.

When we awakened the next morning, the news was frightening: Yeltsin had decided to challenge the hard-liners, and tanks were bombarding the White House. We had Katya's phone number but she didn't speak English. It was hours before we found our Russian-speaking friend. He reached Katya's mother, who assured us that Steven and Tom were safe with them. Katya's parents were divorced, but because of the housing situation they lived in the same apartment and shared the same bed. They gave this bed to Steven and Tom; Katya's mother crowded in with Katya in the room she shared with her brother; her father slept on the floor in his studio. I'll never forget their kindness.

After that start, Steven wrote that he and Tom found an apartment in a safe neighborhood. He began to look for work.

Around Thanksgiving, we received a letter from Tom's father. "Dear Mr. and Mrs. Mackey, I thought you should have this." The note was attached to a copy of a letter from Tom to his parents. I no longer have it, but I read and re read it until I memorized its contents. It offered information that Steven had kindly withheld:

> Dear Mom and Dad. Steve and I are fine. We got to the airport and asked ourselves "Now what do we do?" So we called Katya and she came to get us and we went to her house. They gave us their bed to sleep in, and in the morning Katya's mother asked "Did you hear anything last night?" But we were so tired we didn't hear a thing. Then she told us that tanks had been going down the street in front of their apartment all night long so we decided to see what it was about. We went down to send you a fax but tanks were surrounding Central Telegraph and we couldn't get near. Then we decided to get something to eat and went to the Arbat to look for McDonald's. While we were having breakfast we heard bullets, and decided to get out of there. Later on we went over to the bridge with Katya, and watched the shelling. We found a place to live in, a good neighborhood, and will move in soon. Love, Tom."

Apparently, Steven was now launched in Russia, where he eventually settled for seven years. Grandpa would have been excited, had he known his descendant was witnessing a Russian power play, and would be participating in the daily life of a Muscovite. Grandpa would have said, "Write about it."

CHAPTER 30

My First Russian Scenes

———

I STEPPED OFF THE PLANE at Sheremeteyevo Airport after a two-hour flight from Amsterdam, where my long-standing friend Georgie had joined me. We moved along the gray-green corridor, descended stairs, and joined the mob at passport control. I looked up at the ceiling. Thick fibrous dust hung from openings in the ventilation system. Alert young men stood against walls, holding rifles aslant their chests. One stepped forward when I mistakenly crossed a yellow line painted on the floor. I jumped back.

A sole passport window was open for all foreign arrivals. As the crush grew worse, more windows opened, one at a time, each managed by an officer who scrutinized documents without expression. When I reached the window, the official met my nod and smile with a signal that meant "Hand them over." He recorded my data, returned my passport and visa, and waved me on. I felt menaced and fearful. I didn't know about the firm division between public and private in Russian culture. Friendliness is reserved for trusted family and friends; other relationships are formal and business-like: "correct." Smiling at an official violates a boundary.

Steven was committed to living in Russia for the 1993-94 year; I thought it my one opportunity to visit. In January I had called Georgie, who lived in Holland, and we began to plan our April trip: half a week in Moscow, half in St. Petersburg. Georgie read several guidebooks, made a vocabulary list, and talked with tour agencies. She had traveled more than I, and had developed solid instincts. I bought a guidebook, flipped through it, purchased a map of Moscow, and agreed long-distance with Georgie's ideas. Now we were about to fulfill some of those plans.

Steven's work as an Embassy security guard prevented his meeting our plane, so we had arranged for transfers. We knew that "someone holding a sign with our names" would meet us. We pushed through the crowd and found a young woman in brown, with dark-rimmed glasses, black hair pulled back, a serious expression, and a sign saying "Maki-Mklan." She, too, seemed "correct" while escorting us to a van, but became more welcoming as she responded to our questions.

She made an effort to show us our first look at historic sites. We passed the sculpture of a tank barrier, situated on the main road from the airport. It marks the spot where the Russian Army turned back the Germans in the World War II Battle of Moscow. She showed us the monument to Astronaut Yuri Gagarin: a steel needle arcing into the sky. We had our first glimpse of Red Square at night with St. Basil's Cathedral lighted at the far end. We squealed and exclaimed throughout the drive.

When we left the van at our hotel, our elderly driver bowed deep, his hand nearly sweeping the ground. This gesture from Old Russia means, "I welcome the Spirit," and is used while entering and departing from churches. I said to our guide, "We would like to give him a tip."

"No. It is not our custom."

We were in Russia! It was Reagan's "Evil Empire," the land of reputed automatons, the country of my grandfather's romance with economic justice. In the movie "Reds," John Reed reports from Russia in 1917: "I have seen the future and it works." (This insertion into the script referred to a 1921 quote from the muckraker Lincoln Steffens.) Emma Goldman in the same movie: "It's not working!"

Change was going on, mostly invisible to us. This was not my grandfather's idealized Lenin-led revolution, but – as in Lenin's time – there was hope, pain and corruption. Grandpa, who saw the hope, would have tried to engage everyone in conversation. He would have described his encounters in his newspaper column. I was content to observe, with Steven escorting us when he could.

It was wonderful to see him looking happy, healthy, and confident. I expected more facility in the language and familiarity with Moscow, but I don't know why. Living as a newcomer in an unfamiliar environment is exhausting. Still, he took us to eat in a new restaurant, on a Moscow River houseboat. We sat at a wooden table next to the window, ate mushroom turnovers, and watched the buildings along the river turn pink, then blue, as the sun set. (My memory of this is very clear, but Steven has told me it took place in 1998.) We took him to the American Bar and Grill where the lengthy wait felt worthwhile, because both salmon and vegetables were fresh. It was so expensive that I wondered *could Russians afford this?*

He led us through dark dorm hallways in Moscow State University. Light bulbs were rare in these premier University's imposing Stalin Era buildings. He took us to Lenin's tomb. Once, lines had extended around Red Square. Now they were short. The soldiers' demeanors were serious and stiff. We maintained silence as we circled the corpse on its bed, suit on, hands crossed, beard trimmed. Lenin's skin shone with a fluorescent cast.

From these outings, several moments are so bright that I shall retain them always. In the first, I see us on our way to Gorky House, the Art Nouveau house where Maxim Gorky – early Revolutionary and later cultural spokesman – lived during the thirties. Although it's April, the streets are still being cleaned. Bits and piles of black frozen snow are here and there; the melting snow has left mud everywhere. Steven, Georgie, and I pick our way toward a street sign to discover our location, map in hand. The map is recent, but streets are being re-named every day, Soviet names dropped, and pre-Revolutionary names revived. Every venture turns into an exploration.

Curbside, on one of these shifting streets, we see a destroyed car. The front end is exploded out, and the finish burned off to the underlying steel grey. A bomb had gone off during the previous week. The pop star owner survived, but his driver lost both legs. Because this was an early incident in the gang wars, it made the papers. The sudden change from state to private ownership – economic "shock therapy" – was exacting its price.

Now, near the car's ugly shell, we enter Gorky House. We are the only visitors, and can take our time. But first we put on felt over-slippers, which protect floors. After we strap them on, we begin to see our surroundings. I'm mesmerized by the curves – along the staircase, in stained-glass windows, in decorative tiles on fire-place mantels or stove chimneys, in leaf and vine-like elements of plasterwork. We could be in a Guimard-designed house in Paris. Our eyes feast everywhere.

Another moment: after leaving Gorky House, we walk into the Metro entrance and down the stairs. A woman is cleaning the steps, her kerchief knotted under her chin, her head curved down toward her task. She looks old, but could be young and worn out. She's kneeling on the steps, concentrating on her work. She has no tools. With one chapped, bare hand she sweeps up the debris: cigarette butts, dried spit, used Metro tickets. She pushes this crud into her other hand. I walk on past her, down the stairs, heading for dinner in a restaurant. Then I realize what I've seen. I feel sick.

When I see her in my mind, I'm appalled. Did she once possess tools, which became stolen? Was she supposed to supply her own? Had she lost her job in the economic turmoil? Was her pension so devalued she had to supplement her income this way? And why didn't I give her some rubles?

I learned that swift economic changes and rampant inflation brought poverty to retired Russians. Before privatization, a person could retire with a nice apartment and a comfortable pension – at least, in the cities. Now these pensions had little value. We saw Pensioners lining Metro exits or sitting at nearby tables, holding out a puppy, a box of spaghetti, old books, a necklace, table linens – bits of family history for sale, in order to live in the present.

In the final moment, the three of us are walking in Red Square. We see a group of about twenty-five older people. They're waving red flags and banners. This scene is familiar to Steven, and he keeps on walking, but Georgie and I are curious and move closer. Suddenly we're surrounded. Someone steps closer, shouting into my face in English: "Go back! Go back to America where you belong! We don't want you!" I'm shaking in adrenalin-charged fear. There's no point in "engaging in dialogue" or "attempting an empathic connection" – skills I tried to practice in my professional life. We look around, find an opening in the crowd and head toward Steven. He's turned back to find us. It's a relief to see his open face. He says, "Well, Mom, you just met some retired Communists."

This is not Grandpa's dream country.

CHAPTER 31

Crossing Boundaries

———

AFTER OUR 1994 VISIT, GEORGIE and I returned to our homes and work (hers as a therapist, mine as a pastor). I began to read Russian history. I hadn't anticipated this fascination – it was as though a cork was removed, releasing effervescence everywhere. Steven returned to Massachusetts to work, improve his language skills, and earn a master's degree. Then he seized the opportunity to work full-time in Russia for International Research and Exchanges Board (IREX), a non-governmental organization. (Later, while working there, he would meet Olga, his future wife.) He told me he'd wanted to be part of Russia's own "Yes, we can!"

Georgie, Steven, and I met on the platform of Novoslobodskaya station. Bright August sunlight was dancing through Art Deco stained glass and landing on marble walls and floors. Steven had arrived from his apartment near the Circle Line; Georgie and I had walked from our home stay. (We always moved quickly past the muddy corner, home to several listless, abandoned, hungry dogs.) We three boarded the train and rode to the line's end.

Because IREX sponsored our visa, Steven had asked if we were willing to meet with a group of women in Yaroslavl to discuss women's issues. Given our feminist convictions, he'd found the right hook. Some of these women had participated in one of his programs, which fostered professional development for mid-career people by placing them in American internships.

Now we were on our way to Yaroslavl. We left the Metro station and crossed the plaza to purchase our train tickets. Soon we were standing in a Russian line: three people ahead of us, each holding places for several unknowns, forty-five minutes of shifting weight from one leg to the other, and plenty of time to speculate. Who would be in the group of women we were going to meet? Steven didn't know. Irina, a graduate of his program, was organizing the gathering. It was because she'd mentioned starting a women's club that he had offered Georgie and me as resources.

Although Georgie and I were alert to women's issues, we wondered what we could provide for the unknown mix of participants. Georgie's style was to gather as much information and ideas as possible, and decide at the last minute. I like plans. I came up with three questions to shape conversation, which I took from a Russian movie: "What do you love? What do you fear? What do you hope for?" Irina was polite during our one phone conversation, but uninterested in this approach. Georgie and I continued to speculate until the time came to find the platform and board our train.

Each of us settled into the rhythm of the mostly silent four-hour trip. Travelers employ the word "vast" to describe the Russian countryside; it's a necessary word. We rode through birch forests and saw farm machinery rusting in fields. I spotted a man sitting next to watermelons stacked in a pile the size of three cords of wood. It was his income for the coming year, I felt sure.

As I dreamed out the window, I wondered what my grandfather might say had he known of this journey. Because he'd followed Russian events, our dinnertime conversations at home moved from backyard green beans, to neighborhood news, to Russian sacrifice during World War II. (This was before the McCarthy Era dampened our talk). He would have used strong words about income distribution to describe the man with watermelons. He would have been enraged that Russia was suffering from high inflation, even though it was better than in 1994. Grocery stocks were still thin. Yeltsin's devaluation of the ruble had wiped out savings and pensions.

Irina met our train, settled us in our hotel, and gave us the address for our gathering. "We're celebrating the opening of a new school year," she told us, and mentioned that we'd have two hours for our conversation before it was time for zakuskii, the appetizers that begin every meal. She left us with plans to meet later. After a rest, we changed clothes, and made our short walk to the meeting spot.

We three checked in with a security guard, crossed the courtyard punched through by goose grass, and approached a metal door under a corrugated awning. Rust was everywhere. Chunks of concrete had crumbled off the steps. I looked at Steven: was this place safe? He was at ease; apparently everything was normal.

As dark-haired Irina greeted us, she led us into the stale-tobacco bar near the banquet room. In the crowded space, a circle of chairs was arranged close to the barstools. Women were assembling – young and middle-aged, made up and dressed up.

About twenty-five of us gathered, all but one fluent in English. We introduced ourselves and began to talk about consciousness-raising groups, which encouraged American women to work for expanded legal rights. We described circles of women meeting to speak honestly, rather than to repeat what we were *supposed* to think and feel. I referred to 1968 as a tragic point in America: the assassinations of Martin Luther King, Jr. and Bobby Kennedy, the riots and police action at the Democratic National Convention.

Georgie described what we had learned in Moscow about research and resources available to Russian women.

But it's our beginning introductions that I still ponder in my heart. Georgie was first. She spoke about starting a women's center in The Netherlands, with services for refugees and abused women. As I looked around the circle, I saw welcoming eyes, questioning half-frowns, curious smiles.

Then it was my turn. I might have mentioned my work as a pastor. I told them about my grandfather's enthusiasm for the Russian Revolution, his early support of Lenin, his commitment to economic equality, and my discovery of his 1936 pamphlet "On the Success of the Russian Experiment." (This isn't the correct title, but that's how I remembered it.)

Faces around the circle snapped shut.

Grandpa wouldn't have noticed – he was always focused on his dreams for ideal community. And *I* almost missed their reaction: I felt it, but didn't comprehend.

Now I realize this was more than a *faux pas* – I had crossed a boundary. At the time, I wanted to connect with these women. But they were Capitalists-in-training. Our worlds had changed, yet I presumed they might want to speak about their tragic history. Every so often I'd been able to speak about *my* heritage. But that didn't mean *they* should do so. Each of them must have known about family members who had been repressed. Whatever loss was held in that room was not to be exposed, at least not in that setting, and not by my initiative.

The women were gracious, however, and introductions continued. A young blond woman spoke: "I studied for a year at Stonehill College in Massachusetts, and now I teach a course in women's psychology." She claimed all the scholarly papers we had brought to pass around.

"I have the Mary Kay franchise for this area," said another. My mouth opened in surprise: *Mary Kay in Yaroslavl!*

A tall woman, with high cheekbones and long hair, was matter-of-fact: "I'm a typical victim. I want to work, and whenever I accept a job, my husband calls my employer and has me fired." The other women nodded, sharing their support for her job search.

"I spent six weeks in a Vermont travel agency, and six more at a college, and now I've opened my own language school." This was the competent Irina.

When another woman spoke, she flung bitter words toward us: "I wish *my* mother could go to *your* country but there is no money." I couldn't reply; Georgie leaned forward to say that she, too, wanted travel for that mother.

The freedom of travel is a privilege, even if gained by personal thrift and careful planning. Observing others and interacting with them does provide surface connections. But that's almost voyeurism. I wanted to know more. Now my questions changed from those I had claimed from the Russian movie. I wanted to ask: how do your children fare? What are your hopes and fears for your country? How did you learn to question and doubt? I wanted to hear these stories, but there was no time to develop the bedrock trust required.

In my family, my grandfather's politics had brought whispers, half-sentences, silence, an erosion of trust. His enthusiasms became a family secret – something known but rarely mentioned, and not discussed. It took me years to want to decode the silence, to unravel secrets, to sort through stories, as I'm doing now. It takes time to re-form these stories into the new, complex, and richer understanding that results. I'm grateful to that circle of women in Yaroslavl for their contribution to my story.

The last woman to introduce herself was volunteering at the local paper, hoping and waiting for a paid position. She told us "We have decided that if anything is to change in this country, it will be up to the women." She was large and comfortable-looking. She gave me a warm look, a genuine laugh, and said that she'd enjoyed hearing about my grandfather's support of Lenin.

It felt like a kind of forgiveness.

CHAPTER 32

Bright Glade

———

THE PATH ENTERING YASNAYA POLYANA winds up a long slope. Sunshine dives through tall, tall birches, splashing the walk beneath their branches. Someone planted these thin white trees years before, on both sides of the gravel way. Now they tower; their leaning habit forms them into arches. It's a cloister-approach splattered with gold. I still see this entrance, as if we had just arrived that day in 2001.

Before entering, after we got off the tour bus, I saw the red chicken. She could have been an official greeter for the Great Estate, but was busy hunting for bugs. Dylan tried to get close to her, calling "Corricoroo, corricoroo." My grandson, nearly eighteen months old, loved that word "corricoroo." The hen moved. He called, she moved; we smiled.

About twenty-five of us strolled up the gravel way. We moved in small groups, breathing good air far from Moscow, which was polluted by August peat fires burning to the city's north. I saw a large pond on our left; across, a small log hut was planted among bright shrubs and trees. This cabin looked as peaceful as the pond waters. I wondered if Tolstoy struggled, trying to live a primitive life in this retreat. Or was he so focused on reinventing himself as a peasant that he felt no conflict with his life as a noble? I didn't try to answer these questions. Instead, a sense of beauty entered me as we moved toward our goal: the Grand House at the top of the slope.

I had wanted to see Yasnaya Polyana – "Bright Glade" in English – for many years. Some say it's the home of the world's greatest novelist. It was also a pilgrimage point for those drawn to Tolstoy's views of simplicity and peace – Jane Addams in 1896, William Jennings Bryan, a leading Democratic politician, in 1903. Addams and Bryan were influences on Progressive politics in the United States, and both had spoken at the Saturday Lunch Club. Grandpa would have wanted to join the pilgrimage.

I asked Steven to buy a tour for my visit. My daughter-in-law Olga did the search, and one day we all got on the bus together: Steven, Olga, Dylan, Babushka Tanya – Dylan's other grandmother – and I, "Grandma Janet." During the three hours' drive, when Dylan slept on my lap, I crooned to him.

"Mom. Quiet." *Why is Steven shushing me? I'm not belting out nursery rhymes.* He gave the same response to my question: "Shhh." At last he whispered: "Olga purchased a Russian tour. Don't speak English." I was still puzzled.

We arrived at the Grand House and saw the long porch where Tolstoy's children had played. We smiled at my first grandchild, as he climbed steps and led the way right to the front door. We put on the felt over-slippers designed to protect floors, and followed the tour guide, who pointed to the drawing room with its horse-hair furniture and piano. Her exposition was detailed, lengthy, nuanced, and entirely in Russian. The meaning of "Russian tour" sank in. Steven wouldn't be translating for me, lest he be overheard. I took Dylan outside.

Later, Steven explained that because thrifty Olga had purchased a Russian tour, I had to be a temporary illicit Russian. Foreigners pay higher admission prices, and are excluded from Russians tours. Were it reported that the guide had accepted me, she could be fined, perhaps lose some livelihood. My presence required that I become mute.

I later learned about a dining table where Tolstoy's friends, fellow authors and neighboring nobles talked into the night. I heard that Mme. Sophia Tolstoy sat at the wooden writing table to copy "War and Peace" seven times over, until she demanded that the master stop his corrections. I was told about the children's beds around the corner and down the hall. But I never saw the embroidered cloth on the dining table, the grain of the writing table, or the children's severe cots.

Dylan and I played. I couldn't disguise my loping American gait, but we were hidden from the group. I chased him down the fir tree allée, and listened to him giggle. I watched him conquer the steps of the small schoolhouse, a witness to Tolstoy's project for serf children. I prevented his drinking from a community metal cup hanging on the pump. I picked him up when he stumbled into a flowerbed, carried him to the lawn, and always returned his gorgeous smile.

I saw nothing of the Grand House, learned nothing about Yasnaya Polyana on that all-Russian tour. But when sunshine dove through the birches, it splashed all over us. Oh, it was a golden, golden day.

CHAPTER 33
Cold Water Celebration

———

IT'S A JULY EVENING IN Moscow, 2002. I'm holding my month-old granddaughter Jessica, and she is screaming.

No one knows why – she'd napped well, nursed very well, and burped enthusiastically.

Perhaps it's the company, maybe the crowded apartment. Although the hallway is wide, the living room is small – even after furniture was pushed back to accommodate a dozen guests. We're all here for a first look at our newest family member. It's a tradition: no one but immediate family may see a newborn infant until a month has passed. Then there's a party for relatives and close friends.

Another Russian tradition is also in force at the same time: the annual hot water pipe cleaning and inspection. The hot water is shut off for one month every summer, in all apartment buildings in Moscow, on a rotating schedule. Those who live here become used to this – I once heard Steven refer to "Americans complaining about cold showers." Olga had come home from the hospital to their cold-water apartment with three-day-old Jessica in her arms.

She accepted the situation. In the following days, she used the electric teakettle and three large pots. These sat on the stove's burners with simmering water. She heated water for Dylan and Jessica's daily baths. She heated water for washing dishes, cooking pots, and utensils. She heated water for daily laundry, and for housekeeping. Her mother Tanya, and Steven, did their share of filling, heating, and emptying, filling, heating, and emptying pots.

I arrived three days before Jessica's party and I, too, pitched in. I changed the ever-blossoming pile of dirty dishes into clean small piles draining on the tiny rack in the cramped kitchen. I dried them, returned them to cupboards, and started over on the large pile.

The night before the party, Olga baked a nine-layer cake, using her one round cake pan nine times over. She mixed batter while the previous layer cooled and the dirty pan soaked. She cleaned the dirty pan with the kettle's hot water, poured in batter for the second layer, baked it, iced the first layer, and began again. It must have taken her most of the night. She didn't even look tired, but retained her beauty: brown eyes, high cheekbones, slender build, and long, curly, barely-tamed hair.

Besides the cake, there were other preparations. Steven asked me to make devilled eggs, not familiar to Russians, but a favorite of Steven's. Babushka Tanya arrived with her eggplant-garlic-tomato-sour cream appetizers. These were set out on the living room table among other platters of food – kabobs, salads, sausages, and bread.

It's time to celebrate. As guests arrive they choose foods randomly, or so it seems to my American eyes. Some pull up a chair up at the table, others walk around with plates in hand.

In the background, people talk, music plays, and Jessica screams. We take turns holding her and walking around. Sometimes she drops off to sleep on a shoulder and then awakens again. I develop a technique of thumping her on the back in rhythm. *Thump-thump. Thump-thump-thump.* Tanya walks past me and shakes her finger at me in a "stop that" gesture. (An older Jessica will come to love this part of the story.) But my thumping works to quiet her, so I continue. Jessica goes to sleep. I hand her over to Tanya and attend to more dishes.

Then, at about ten pm: "We have hot water!" That's Olga. I've never greeted dirty dishes with such happiness. The guests continue to eat and drink, I continue to wash dishes. As the evening ends, so do two Russian traditions new to me: the annual hot-water shut off and the only coming out party for infant Jessica.

CHAPTER 34
Hide and Seek

─────

WHEN I SAT ON MY son's balcony in Moscow – it was 2012, my first visit to Russia in several years – I looked straight into a birch grove. If before lunch, I watched preschoolers tumble around trees and down the slope. After school, 'tweens replaced them, playing in bubbling water, a supply meant for hose hook-ups. In spring twilight, middle-schoolers socialized.

He and his family were living in housing for Embassy employees, but this gated enclave reminded me of the Village of Morningside in Minnesota, where I lived for three childhood years. It was safe. Streets flowed with children sitting in baby carriages, riding on tricycles, or flying by on scooters. Still others ran among houses, passed the water fountain, and wove through birch trees playing Hide and Seek.

Because of secure boundaries, children's energies became unleashed. Parents gathered and watched them as shashliks cooked on the grill. They told each other: "Remember this. Savor this." They blessed each other: "We're so fortunate – you don't get this everywhere. This is rare." That's how it was with my grandparents' home on Alden Drive.

There *are* differences. Morningside wasn't enclosed. We weren't required to wear a badge, nor to escort visitors. Townhouses of the nineties faced these streets, not the shingled, stucco, or bungalow homes of the thirties and forties. The street lamps were different, too. In this Moscow compound, they looked more like lamps of Old Virginia, or Boston's Beacon Hill – the kind one sees in illustrations of Victorian stories.

And there were the second set of lamps: white casings on top of black poles, containing bulbs pointing down, the housing vented on two sides. I never saw one lighted. They're meant to be jarring.

On the first day of my April visit, Steven pointed out the front window to one of these fixtures. "The FSB installed these cameras just a month ago." (FSB is the current version of the Russian secret police.)

"Are they everywhere?" I asked him, fascinated by the thing.

"No. Just the American section." His tone was light.

"Then I suppose this whole place is wired." I meant our living quarters.

"Oh, yes. Tiny cameras everywhere. We're not supposed to look for them."

I stopped. Wouldn't my observations and questions get recorded, too? I wondered how I *could* get more information. I decided to ask questions during walks *outside* the community, where there are no cameras. Twenty-four hours after arriving at Sheremeteyevo Airport, I had to rein in my curiosity.

Something interrupted us, and I filed away the admonition to avoid looking for hidden cameras. But I developed the eye-sweep. I couldn't stop. Even if I tried a casual motion of my head, there was a lurch in the stomach, a tingle in the shoulder.

"What's that?" I didn't mean to ask my granddaughter Jessica, but I did anyway. We were sitting in the living room, near one of the Wi-Fi hot spots. I pointed to a light switch with a glowing red dot. It stood alone, next to a bank of three switches in the dining room.

"Just a special light." She smiled, and returned to her text messages.

One morning, Jessica asked me why I went out every day. "It's silly to be in Moscow…" I began, but she put her finger to her lips. "This is what we do," she said. *Steven must have prepped the children. Jessica thinks I'm going to slander Russians.* I repeated, "It seems silly to be in Moscow and not explore museums and neighborhoods." She nodded and took another bite of her Nutella-smeared breakfast bread.

By this time, I'd noticed straight trenches dug through lawns in the American section, overlaid with bits of sod. The work looked sloppy; the grass wasn't healing very fast. These trenches led directly from the FSB cameras, and must contain wires. The FSB has a purpose: *"We're here."* No one commented on them. It felt as though my family lived on two levels: one of daily routine, and another of minor alertness hovering above breakfast, after-school friendships, evening TV, and bedtime conversation. I remained on one level -- alert.

As April turned to May, friends came over for snacks on a Friday evening. As we passed food around, Steven cupped his hands around his mouth, looked at the ceiling, raised his voice, and said, "If you're listening. . . . "

"Don't. Don't, Steve." Sharon looked at him. "Our neighbors came home the other day and found all their condiments turned upside down."

"How long were you here before it started?" Steven asked Brad, Sharon's husband.

"About six months. Mostly phantom phone calls, sometimes early in the morning. The phone rings. No one's there."

I wanted to learn more, but didn't ask, since someone was either listening or watching. It's as if my conscience had dressed up in a uniform, observing me on a monitor. But what was I guilty of?

The next morning I was alone, and there were two phantom phone calls. One had office noises in the background.

Several days later, while walking home with groceries, I broached the subject with Steven. He treated it as a game. "They retaliate. If you're riding a bicycle and think you're being followed, and you weave in and out of traffic to shake them, then the next day your bike is gone. Or you might come home one day to find that someone's taken a dump in your toilet." We arrived at the gate. "It's probably no big deal," he added. "If we had some Embassy guests over and they heard us complaining about the Ambassador, then they might turn the cameras on." *So they're always recording, but not always watching.*

One day, Dylan came home from school. "My rip-stick's been stolen. And what gets me is, I wasn't careless. I didn't just leave it somewhere. Someone had the nerve to walk up to the house and just take it from the entrance." He became absorbed in a video game. I knew that the neighborhood kids stored rip-sticks like that. They rode them along the winding streets to the school gate, left them, and rode home after school. It's a safe community, everyone said.

I interrupted his game to suggest we walk around to look for it, or post a sign at the gate. "How would you know if one is yours?" I ask him.

"Every kid rides in a different way," he explained. "You can tell by the way it balances."

On the day before, when my daughter-in-law Olga and I had walked down the street, we passed a man hanging out. I was sure the FSB took the rip-stick. I didn't bring up my suspicion. She hadn't noticed the man; our goal had been to catch the shuttle to the metro.

I began to question details I'd usually ignore. What is that rhythmic high-pitched sound I hear early in the morning? Why does the house have thermostats, when a radiator valve controls the heat? Do the ceiling grills hide microphones and cameras? The overhead light in the kitchen – why is the fixture askew?

The questions always floated around me, but after awhile I lost energy for considering them. I made excursions to Tretyakov Gallery, returned via the grocery store, chopped tomatoes for salad, or sautéed chicken. I went to a presentation by Cold War Ambassador Joseph Davies' granddaughter. We spent a day at an International Fair. We celebrated May Day at Starlite Diner, an ex-pat hangout near Pushkin Square. I heard about plans for Dylan's weeklong school trip to Suzdal, and felt jealous. We joined with Babushka Tanya to explore an old Tsarist estate. We invited family over for Victory Day and feasted all day long. We listened to Jessica play her two recital pieces.

At suppertime one day, Dylan announced that he'd retrieved his rip-stick from an eighth grader, who'd taken it. Olga suggested the phantom phone calls might have been from her mother, who couldn't hear my "Hello? Hello? Hello?" I remained skeptical – I know there were background office noises in one call. I learned that the little red light on the dining room switch indicated a dimmer in use. The sod over the trenches melded into May grass. I began to think I could get used to being recorded. I began to live on two levels, like my family.

But just before my visit ended, Jessica handed me a piece of paper. She'd written "Am I half Russian? Circle One: 'yes' or 'no.'" I started to say, "Of course…"

"Shhhh," she whispered, and leaned into my ear. "We can't talk about this. Write your answer. They're listening. It could hurt Dad's job." Her voice was too soft to hear the rest of her warning.

Back in northern Virginia now, I realize I don't mind cameras at intersections. Instead, I surprise myself with empathy for those FSB agents who'd listened to our exchanges:

"Tomorrow we're going to Kolomenskoye."

"Oh, it's so bo-o-oring. We just walk around and look at old buildings. I want to stay home. I'm old enough."

"Please stop whining. It's important. It's part of your heritage. We're all going."

Or: "Your Russian teacher called and said you used bad language in class."

"Those girls were bugging me, and I told them to 'shut up.' That's not a bad word."

"It is to your Russian teacher. Besides, that's exactly how those girls want you to react. Don't give them satisfaction."

I imagine young men and women sitting at desks, trolling through hours of these exchanges. They're bored. They wonder if they've missed something important. They take a cigarette break and talk about boyfriends or spouses. They leave when a second crew arrives to replace them. At the Metro exit, they buy a meat pie or a sweet roll. They go home to their parents and TV, or they kiss their wife and baby. They ask about supper. They dream about a promotion.

Then I ask myself *who's tracking my emails here in America?* When in Russia, I felt uncomfortable knowing we were watched, but after the first jolt and time's passing, I became used to feeling constrained.

In the USA, I still assume freedom and privacy when I should not. I order a product online, and its cousin shows up, inviting me into another purchase. This seems normal, but it's far removed from Morningside Village, when ordinary gossip was the means of keeping track of others. Or when people read about someone in my grandfather's column.

Sill, there was the McCarthy Era. While I don't recall specifics, I can recollect the atmosphere. Symptoms must have been there, even during the perceived American unity of World War II. The McCarthy time felt like the onset of an unexpected illness. Suspicion and fear once directed against Germany and Japan soon became directed against a new postwar enemy – the Reds.

Dis-ease showed up everywhere. Prominent people were black-listed, including those my grandparents knew. One of these was Grandpa's colleague Marian LeSueur's daughter, Meridel. Her articles about poverty were no longer published, and she lived on the margins by writing children's stories. Dis-ease trickled into our home when my sister Carol was bullied, my brother Dudley beat up, and when Margaret and Dad worried about Grandpa's next letter to the editor. Today I can summon the noxious atmosphere with little effort.

The American atmosphere isn't as hysterical now, as it was then. Yet, knowing that my electronic data is tracked feels eerily similar to knowing about hidden mikes within that safe, gated compound, where I spent time with my family in Moscow.

CHAPTER 35
Russian Easter

———

IT WAS EASTER SUNDAY IN MOSCOW, 2012. The April air warmed me as I stepped over melting ice to climb into the car. Steven, Dylan, and Jessica were already strapped in.

We were heading for a one o'clock feast at Babushka Tanya's home; Olga was already there, helping her mother. As we left through the community's gate, I realized I no longer felt fearful, menaced, and wary. Nine previous trips had increased my comfort level, and I could slip into a different way of doing things. I sometimes joked that with each visit I'd seen less of the country and more of supermarket, kitchen, and playground. Yet, I was still excited. In the nineteen-sixties I had sung "Moscow Nights" with friends, and in the seventies began to reflect about my grandfather's support of Russia and its "new society." But I'd never imagined that one day I'd visit my family here.

We turned onto the highway. Dylan looked up from his smart phone to ask how long we'd be there. He was twelve years old, expert at maneuvering away from family and toward friends. "All afternoon," said Steven.

"Oh, no!" Dylan started to whine.

"Kids." Steven repeated his conviction: "Family time is important. Today is a special meal." His response made me happy. Dylan and Jessica returned to their smart phones, perhaps to text their friends about cruel and unusual punishment.

We arrived. Steven maneuvered the car into a gravel-topped parking lot across the street from the apartment building. As with many Russian buildings, the shabby-looking entrance put me off. Once we were inside the elevator, Jessica shivered: "Grandma, I'm scared of elevators. Babushka Tanya and I got stuck in this one. It just stopped. We yelled and yelled. We had to wait a long time before it started again." I, too, felt relieved when we reached the sixth floor landing.

We entered Tanya's well-kept hallway, removed our shoes, added them to the pile, and straightened up with greetings: "Privyet, Tanya" (the familiar term), and "Zdravstvuite" (the formal "hello") to Tanya's friends. A couple in their eighties, long-standing friends of Tanya's, returned our greetings. The man, tall and thin with rimless glasses and sparse hair, held up a bottle of amber liquid for admiration, while his sparrow-sized wife looked on. "It's brandy he made himself," Olga explained. Mikhail, the other guest who was short and olive-skinned, smiled his welcome. He'd known Olga since their elementary school days, and became a newspaper editor.

When we turned into the all-purpose room, about twenty feet by twelve, we saw Tanya's bed placed against an end wall. A storage cabinet with TV occupied the long wall, and opposite this was a couch, where some of us would sit while feasting. A table and chairs filled all the remaining space. Enticing smells suffused the air.

Tanya, an energetic eighty-two with curly, short, white hair, urges us to table. We crowded into our seats in an arrangement guaranteeing we wouldn't move while eating. But I didn't mind cramped quarters. Nine people around a table evoked memories of holiday meals with my grandparents when we ate food from their garden, and we children overheard adult conversation, which shaped our family's traditions: love for history, concern for justice, and commitment to economic equality.

I carried those dinnertime conversations, from nearly seventy years ago, into Tanya's home that Sunday in Moscow. A white cloth covered Tanya's table, just as one had at my grandmother's. In the middle stood a traditional Easter bread – tall and cylindrical like a chef's hat – with thin white frosting dribbling down the sides. A bottle of vodka held a place next to it. Tanya began by pouring sweet wine into our glasses while telling us – according to Olga – that it's a traditional wine for Easter Sunday. We lifted our glasses to toast. "To the holiday," translated Olga.

A platter of sliced whitefish and salmon sat at the far end of the table. A round dish of lobio (kidney beans, cilantro, walnuts and spices) was within Olga's reach. I spotted a plate of sour black bread, and "gray" bread, similar to American whole wheat. A platter of cold meats – ham, and jellied pork – rested near me. Another dish held crisp cucumber salad. The elderly woman helped herself to several kinds of sausage, while I assessed sliced eggplant. These were zakuskii – the first course.

How different was this table, I reflect, from that at my grandparents' home. There we might have begun with soup on Easter Day, but normally we started with the main course of meat, potatoes, a vegetable, and sometimes salad. "Spirits" and wine were absent – not necessary. At Babushka Tanya's, each person started to eat when in the mood, calling out for a desired food, or reaching across the table to fork it up. At Grandma's table, Grandpa carved the meat and dished it onto a plate. We passed it to Grandma for vegetables, and she then sent it down the other side of the table to a designated person. Pickles, bread, and butter moved around in orderly fashion, left to right. We always waited until everyone was served and Grandma began to eat, before picking up our forks. Today, my grandchildren might think their great-great-grandparents' meals bland and stilted. But conversation about race-prejudice, Cold War wrongs, and Union activities gave spice and liveliness to our dinners.

That style of family feast sticks with me. I love menu planning, choosing ingredients, cooking, the table setting, and the feeling of being *materfamilias* when we're all gathered. It's taken me many Russian meals to become used to a different style. I remind myself that I can't replicate my grandparents' dinnertimes, and insert them into gatherings decades later, or into a different culture away from home. I can't even achieve it in my own home, when my family's with me. How curious it is, that a Russian saying rings true both here in Moscow, and for my Minnesota grandparent's meals: "The tabletop is God's hand. That's why it's important to gather around it."

Tanya brought me out of my reverie when she offered a toast, and we all clinked glasses – the children, too, with their soft drinks. "To family and friendship," reported Steven. Mikhail, who'd started talking before the zakuskii, continued, animated, and "into" his story. Because I knew more food was on the way, I started with small portions and passed up fish, which looked uncooked. Someone offered another toast. I was relieved that women don't have to drink the vodka – we touched the shot glass or wine glass to our lips.

Everyone filled plates a second time. I stopped with an extra spoonful of tasty lobio. Olga asked Mikhail a question, and he continued with his discourse. The elderly couple listened respectfully. Although I'd met both Mikhail and the couple once before, our lack of a common language hampers understanding.

After more than an hour, Olga and Tanya began to clear the table. "Why didn't you eat any fish?" Olga asked me. It turned out it was smoked and delicious. But I lost my chance. It was time for the main course. Meatballs arrived, steaming in their gravy. A large platter of sliced goose came next, followed by potatoes fried in goose fat. A green salad filled a large bowl, and the bread remained. Olga offered a toast. "It's for missing family members," said Steven, and Mikhail continued to share.

I asked for translation because Steven had gone quiet. He was miffed that Mikhail was the only one talking. He summarized: "He's talking about the corruption of the Church and its Patriarch." He turned his head to spear more goose.

"But what about it?" It was my only chance to hear more.

"Oh, you know the story. Someone reported he'd been seen in a meeting, wearing an expensive watch – more expensive than a Rolex. There was a denial: the church published a photo of the Patriarch at the meeting. No watch on his wrist. But there *was* one reflected on the table surface. They forgot to eliminate the reflection when they photo-shopped the picture."

That's the longest translation I received. Most of the time, I observed and read body language. It felt normal to slip in and out of understanding a conversation. When I'm together with Steven's family, we'll all be speaking English. But when an English word won't do the entire family will start speaking Russian. They don't always know they've switched. At Tanya's, I didn't want to interrupt for an update – it seemed rude. I retreated, and watched my mind flow by.

In our previous meeting, I'd learned about Mikhail's courage. His newspaper, begun during Glasnost, had later been banned from one of the Republics of the former Soviet Union. Mikhail responded by printing it outside that country then drove bundles across the border in the middle of the night. I respect his courage – it's like my grandfather's willingness to be outspoken during the Cold War, when he wrote to newspaper editors demanding fair coverage of Russian news.

At four o'clock it was time to take a break. Olga had told me beforehand that we'd "go to church." I pictured an Orthodox worship service – three hours long – and asked if we'd stay for the entire ritual. "No," Olga responded, "we'll just stop in for awhile." I was glad to be going because I'd missed Easter worship in my Virginia church. Since Orthodox Easter was a week later,

I looked forward to hearing *a Capella* music, which soars right through the roof into the atmosphere. Since it seemed unusual to go to worship this late in the day, I wondered if the church held services throughout the day on this most important feast of the Christian year.

We edged our way into the hall, put our shoes back on, and found our way to the nearby church. In the vestibule, Olga purchased enough long thin candles for each of us while I covered my head before entering the sanctuary. No service was in progress. As I carried my taper, I looked around in the quiet. In spite of Mikhail's story of church corruption, serenity invited me.

It was a visual feast. Besides the Iconostasis, there were paintings everywhere. I identified John the Baptist, the Apostle Paul, and an Archangel or two in addition to Christ, and several of Mary – called Theotokos, "God-bearer" – nearly always shown holding Jesus. Icons were on the walls, on stands in front of banks of candles, in corners above small altars. Incense fragrance lingered. I found a Theotokos, lit a candle, and prayed for a friend's son.

Jessica joined me. "Grandma, why didn't you cross yourself? You should. Mom says it's time to go." I didn't see the men. They must have walked in, moved their eyes around, and left. They had to wait outside for the ten long minutes we women were inside. "Going to Church" must have meant, "popping into the Sanctuary." It wasn't what I'd hoped for, yet I felt enriched.

We returned to the apartment and settled into place. It was time for dessert. Someone had replaced the empty vodka bottle with another, but Mikhail reached for brandy instead, still talking. The elderly man offered a toast to the children's future, just as Jessica began to beg her father to allow her to leave the table. "No, Jessica, this is family time. You can hang in."

"Ple-e-e-a-se?" – she was in tears. He relented. Both Jessica and Dylan stretched out face down on Babushka Tanya's bed, dramatizing their suffering.

We divided the cake, listened to Mikhail, and after awhile I sampled a cookie. The elderly woman was in charge of the ceremony of unwrapping and opening a box of chocolates. We each chose one, and I also nibbled at a fruit jelly from another dish.

Now Tanya offered tea; when poured, Mikhail launched into another story. Steven became alert and granted me a quick summary: "He thinks he could be the grandson of one of Stalin's henchmen. The man used to stop by the house and ask 'How are the children? Is everyone alright?'" I whispered to Steven that Mikhail did look like his possible grandfather, whose picture was prominent during the Cold War. Steven agreed.

It was six o'clock and time to leave. Olga and her mother had already cleaned up. Some of the second bottle of vodka was gone, and all of the brandy. We four women were circumspect with wine. I didn't see how the elderly gentleman could stand, but he was steady as a telephone pole. Mikhail, who'd consumed most of the liquor, wasn't swaying either, and his speech seemed as clear as at the start of our visit.

We said our "Paka, Tanya," and "Dosvidanya" several times, as we packed up to go. During our ride home, Dylan summed up. "Mom kept asking questions; Mikhail talked the whole time; Babushka Tanya can't hear, so she just smiled; Dad stared into space; Jessica kept asking 'When can I go to sleep?' and Grandma Janet" – he imitated me by bobbing his head back and forth – "Grandma looked over there, and then here, trying to understand. I asked her why she did that, and she said 'I like to follow.'" He grinned at his irony, and so did I.

It occurs to me that I might have paid my grandchildren to translate for me. They might have been more engaged with conversation through helping me. But perhaps the talk slipped into them on a slant, just as Grandpa's stories had done with me. Maybe they'll awaken to the content when older, just as I'm remembering my grandparents' interests in history and politics. Maybe Jessica will write about it some day, as I attempt to do.

The meal had lasted five hours, with overflowing food, plenty of time to enjoy various tastes, and the promise of interesting conversation. Tanya's hospitality confirmed all the stories I'd heard about Russian welcome. She, who lives in a tiny apartment on a meager pension, lavished food upon us. It wasn't the orderly style of my grandparents' Midwestern household, but it had its own rituals. We didn't go to church in the way I'm accustomed to worship – this isn't a practicing family, after all – but I'm beginning to see beauty that inheres in ancient icons. I didn't understand what Mikhail had to say, although I was fascinated that any one person could hold forth for so much time. It's dangerous to be an outspoken newspaperman in Russia today. Since knowledge is currency in the newspaper world, then he, too, was generous, in his way – sharing all his stories and insight with anyone who'd listen.

As for me, I remain amazed that Grandpa's "travel-itus gene" has taken hold in my family, bringing me to unexpected places and glimpses of cultures beyond the Midwest. In my own way, I've fulfilled Grandpa's interest in Russia. Each year since my first visit in 1994, I've read books and articles about Russia, and Russian news in daily papers. Each time I visited, I made excursions into Moscow to take in museums, view stately buildings, and enjoy city neighborhoods.

I hadn't realized, when I first stepped into those new territories, that my entire family, from my great-grandfather all the way to my grandchildren, would be gathered around the same Easter table, bringing me so much happiness. And the missing are always present, held together by the tabletop that is God's hand.

CHAPTER 36

A Family Founding Story

———

STORIES ABOUNDED DURING DINNERTIMES AT Grandma and Grandpa's, when my dad, siblings, and I lived with them in the nineteen-forties. Grandpa began with his versions, then Grandma or Dad might amplify, question a detail, or contribute another one. Some of these reminiscences must have bored us children, so our minds wandered as we focused on our food. Stories drifted into us.

"I ran into Waldo Emerson, and he said that someone's going to build…."

"Yesterday at the Saturday Lunch Club, there were catcalls…."

"Henry's tomatoes are already ripe, but when I asked about the variety…."

We overheard these stories without focusing on them. The adults didn't direct them to us; they told them for *all* of us, to remind our entire family about our history, our traditions, our self-understanding. Overheard stories are powerful because they enter us by a slant and overcome resistance to the values they carry. Emily Dickinson pointed to this when she wrote, "Tell . . . the truth, but tell it slant." During dinnertime, our grandparents' stories nourished our identities while their food fed our growing bodies.

Great-Grandfather Henry William was the subject of a significant Parsons story. When I puzzle over Grandpa's behavior, or when I wish I could emulate it, I remind myself that Grandpa, too, had parents. Grandpa, too, was handed a legacy: his father's radical views. And the Rev. Henry William Parsons had acted on his beliefs.

That's how I think of him: "the Reverend."

I never knew my great-grandfather, but when I look at his picture, I see a stern man. The photo is a formal one, full face. His beard is impressive; he doesn't smile. If I were to meet him, I wouldn't seek a hug. I would avoid being pinned into place by those eyes. If I were sure of my righteousness, his eyes would question it; if I knew my sins, they would convict me. I have another informal snapshot, in which his six-foot-four-inch frame towers over his plump wife Sarah. His height commands attention. They stand at the side of a house.

My father didn't describe his memories of the Reverend to me. But two stories indicate Henry William's legacy to my grandfather and to the rest of us. Stories that can become a burden or a willing cause. Of Henry's seven living children, my grandfather, fifth in line, took up the legacy with his enthusiastic, optimistic, extroverted temperament.

The first story was well honed. While serving a Congregational church in Brighton, England, Great-Grandfather became a leader in The Independent Order of Good Templars, a society of Lodges committed to total abstinence. This affiliation was a break from his past, for his own father Giles Parsons had lost their home, Gueneford Farm, because of alcoholism. Thus, Henry William's temperance work became a new foundation for our family.

The Templars commissioned him to preach Temperance in the southern United States for three months, so he left his wife Sarah (pregnant with my grandfather) in the fall of 1876. "I am sure you will reconcile yourself to my absence when you think of the Noble Mission on which I am bound," he wrote to her in late October.[65]

After orientation in New York and Philadelphia, a Bishop of the African Methodist Episcopal Church provided letters of introduction for "the Reverend." He then took the train to North Carolina and made a preaching circuit in New Bern, Charlotte, and nearby towns. The setting of the main event varies in different recitals of the story, but an essential fact never changes: he preached mostly to African Americans, occasionally to groups that included white men (perhaps there to check him out). As Uncle Edgar once said to me, "As an Englishman he didn't know you weren't supposed to do that." But he had answered the call, so he focused his piercing eyes on the work of Temperance – the radical work of reforming a dissolute culture.

One day in Charlotte, ruffians followed him, an event he described in a letter to Sarah:

> I was followed after coming out of a meeting which I had attended – by a crowd of some forty or fifty Southerners armed with bludgeons - among them was the City or what would be in England the Chief of Police and the Mayor who charged me with doing that which was detrimental to their race by holding meetings among the colored race – I could see my life was in danger with an infuriated Mob around me so I requested the Mayor with his officer to come to my apartments where I would converse with him on this matter. This they did the Mob following but were not permitted to enter the House. The Scene that was Witnessed in that room is too fearful for me to describe to you – I send you a paper where you will see how unpleasantly I have been brought before the Public here – Never mind all things will work together for good – They cannot harm me if God be on my side. I had to go into the Woods to sleep the last night to save my life I hope the Christian home will pray that I might be preserved to carry this struggle through – the poor Negro is treated here like dust beneath the White man's feet.[66]

According to Grandpa's own memoir, an African American family named Dudley sheltered Henry William, whose obituary says "he continued to eat and drink with Negroes until he could leave town with dignity."

Our grandparents told this story more than once at dinnertime. Other family members referred to it, or repeated it, but I don't recall embellishment – it was like a memorized liturgy that became instruction for a holy vocation. It was our legacy, our lesson: no prejudice against African-Americans was allowed, nor, it was frequently added, American Indians or Jews. (Later, I realized, we held prejudice against Southerners and Catholics.)

Grandpa wrote in his memoir "the Reverend" instructed Sarah after the incident that if the new baby was a boy he must be named Dudley. Did Grandpa recognize the hidden mandate in the story he repeated and repeated? Grandpa's inheritance of social concern was ratified by his name, fostered by his parents, and solidified when he married Clara Dickey, whose father had fought in the Civil War with the Second Minnesota Regiment.

Grandpa was the first generation of "Ernest Dudleys." My father, E. Dudley, Jr., told me the second story about Henry William many years after I heard the first. We were sitting at the kitchen table in the Brookside Terrace house. He launched into it suddenly, as if he had discovered it under his coffee cup. "He would go to a town and advertise a slide show, Janet – the subject was the Franco-Prussian War. He used a projector lighted by a chemical reaction: a flame was directed to a small pillar of calcium carbonate, which is lime. This produced an intense white light. Hence the term *lime-light*," my science-loving father explained.

We were watching the birds at the feeder near the urn and rose garden as he talked. "After these, he brought out another set, called *Ten Nights in a Bar-Room*. These slides demonstrated to the unsuspecting audience their fate if they continued to drink. Then, he would preach the evils of alcohol and form a new Lodge for the Templars."

After I heard that story, years passed until my brother Dudley (the third "Dudley") and my sister-in-law Peg visited me in 2008. They brought family papers – "the Reverend's" diaries and letters from 1873-1887. The pile was heavy and daunting. Dad had placed each sheet into an archival sleeve, and into a binder for each year. Water had damaged some pages, and mice had chewed some corners, so I was surprised to see how bright the ink was in most places.

When I read these papers, I concluded that ritual recitals of the founding story didn't acknowledge certain aspects of Great-Grandfather's personality. That he'd been zealous in the cause of Temperance was clear. It led him to travel in the Mediterranean and southern England, as well as the three months in North Carolina. Temperance work, however, couldn't support his large family of five living children. (Others were born after immigrating to the United States.) His primary call was to be a pastor.

After he returned from North Carolina to England in 1876, he escorted the Fisk Jubilee Singers on their third concert tour of England. But "the Reverend" met difficulties. Some singers seemed demanding and uncooperative. Some apparently got drunk. Whether most problems were due to differences in culture, or due to my Great-Grandfather's personality, I can't say.

He must have been hard to work with – his diaries include notes of attempts to get along with church leaders and of seeking positions elsewhere. There is a tone of "I'm right and they don't understand." "He moved around a lot," my gentle father said. "The Reverend" also wondered how he would find food for his family and worried about a Christmas when he had nothing to give. Somehow he was able to withstand conflict and poverty – he'd been orphaned when nine years old and had made his own way. And he believed in righteous causes.

My having these papers posed at least one problem. Old papers are fragile and require proper storage with controlled humidity. My spare bedroom didn't meet that requirement, but I put them into a closet so I could dither. Then, one day while on a tour of the Library of Congress, it occurred to me that I could donate them to the Library. But would there be interest in these papers? The tour guide said that thousands of submissions arrive each day.

I didn't expect a response to my inquiries, so a phone message from an expert in the manuscript division surprised me. "I'd like to speak with you." When I reached her, she asked for a few details. Then I heard: "We're interested in having these papers because of the connection with the African-American community and for our nineteenth century collection." Done! I checked with my siblings and cousin, dealt with a few formalities, packed and shipped them. At the Library, they'll be digitized and available to anyone interested.

One problem has been addressed: I'm no longer responsible for their care. But what about the legacy they contain? That's still a problem for me. I'm part of the Parsons family. How do I appropriate that Family Founding Story? Shipping the papers didn't rid me of the inheritance: active concern for social justice. It's part identity and part burden. I don't have my grandfather's extroverted personality. So, although I care deeply about social and economic justice, organizing demonstrations or ringing doorbells isn't part of my life. I'm learning to accept that.

Still, each family member has received and used the legacy in a different way. Dad was a strong Union member, loved ideas, and wrote articles about local Edina-Morningside history, which were published in *About Town*, Edina's quarterly magazine. Carol sheltered a family of illegal immigrants and tutored Hispanic speakers. Margaret and Dad took a Cambodian family into their home for six weeks. Dudley goes on service trips each year. Rolf organized politically on behalf of public schools. James transcribed papers and diaries. I worked in the inner city once, and now that I'm retired, I tutor a non-English speaker, but I'm not a "hands-on" organizer.

So I pass on stories.

Biography Notes

Ernest Dudley Parsons, Senior

1876	November 7, Born in England
1882	Arrived in USA with siblings and parents
1886 – 1887	Lived in Madison, Minnesota
1888 – 1891	Lived in Lake Benton, Minnesota
1891 – 1897	Lived in Minneapolis, Minnesota
1898 – 1899	Taught school near Farmington; worked on a newspaper in Stewartville
1899 – 1903	Student at Hamline University, St. Paul, Minnesota
1903 – 1905	Home missionary; pastor at St. Clair and New Richland; also employed at Mankato Congregational Church
1905 – 1907	Principal at Brookings High School, South Dakota
1905	Married Clara Ethel Dickey November 28 in Appleton, Minnesota
1906	Dudley Parsons born December 26
1907 – 1908	Instructor in English, North High School, Minneapolis
1908 – 1928	Instructor in English, West High School, Minneapolis
1908	Purchased first property in Morningside (Edina) Minnesota

1911	Edgar Parsons born January 5
1913	Published *Story of Minneapolis*
1916	Published *Story of Minnesota*; wrote articles for the *Encyclopedia Britannica,* and various newspapers; lectured in northern Minnesota
1916	(and some period of years before) Pastor at North Branch, Elk River, and Minnewashta, Minnesota
1917	Ernest Parsons born October 16
1921	Summer trip to Europe: England, France, and Spain with Clara, Dudley, and Edgar
1925	Bought a Ford and opened an "eatery" on Highway 35, 6 miles east of Danbury, Wisconsin
1926	Published *Making Minneapolis*
1928	Retired from teaching, started to sell insurance; moved into "last house" 4210 Alden Drive, Morningside
1931	Published *Heroes of the Northwest*
1934	Published (with Hugh Curran) *The Government of Minnesota*
1948	Published *Seeing Minneapolis*
1951	Clara Dickey Parsons died
1952	E. Dudley Parsons, Sr. died of pancreatic cancer

Compiled by E. Dudley Parsons, Jr.

Author's Note

———

THIS IS A WORK OF creative nonfiction, begun by setting down memories and impressions, which became disparate stories growing into a pile. It ended as a collage, each unit a weaving of family stories and papers, my grandfather's writing, and historical facts. To the best of my knowledge, what I've set down is accurate, faithful to my own recollections, and checked against historical accounts. I have kept the timeline of my own search to understand my grandfather's impact on our family, to the best of my ability.

An important wellspring for this venture is the trove of letters, diaries, and typescripts, which my grandparents and parents had cared for and left behind. The oldest among these are the diaries and letters of my great-grandfather the Rev. Henry William Parsons, written from 1873 to 1887. These now reside in the Library of Congress, which holds the title but not the copyright, according to Ms. Adrienne Cannon of the Manuscript Division. My brother James Parsons had diligently transcribed the originals; family members have the electronic version of these transcriptions.

Another collection is that of family letters written back and forth from Minnesota to India. I have some of these manuscripts in my possession, and all of them in electronic form, which James had produced. Most of the original letters cannot be found. In the notes and bibliography, I have named them *Parsons Family Letters*. There are other letters as well, outside that particular set.

I have more electronic files (and sometimes typescripts of these also), which James had transcribed from papers now missing. A scrapbook of "Morningsider" columns written between 1935 and 1936 is one of these. My grandfather, E. Dudley Parsons Sr., also wrote a series of notes in the margins of his copy of *The Encyclopedia Britannica*. I have named these *Encyclopedia Britannica Atlas Flyleaf Notes*.

Grandfather Parsons published books, articles, letters to newspaper editors and newspaper columns. The latter appeared in *The Hennepin County Review*, Hopkins, Minnesota. The first columns were named "The Morningsider," and were renamed "Parsonalities" in 1940. The *Review* stopped publishing in 1968. The *St. Louis Park Sun* was its successor, and in 1996 the *Sun* became *The St. Louis Park Sailor*. In 2013, I learned from the *Sailor*'s Senior Managing Editor Mr. Paul Wahl that crediting the original source of newspaper material I use in print is considered sufficient.

Also in my personal collection is a scrapbook of my grandfather's papers, which my father arranged. I refer to this as *E. Dudley Parsons I Scrapbook*. Between the first item (a copy of his birth registration) and the last item (his final passport), this compilation holds newspaper clippings. Most of these are not attributed, nor dated. Whenever possible, I've located the publisher and the date. In some instances, I haven't been able to find the necessary information.

I've been able to include some of the photographs to which I refer. Many were taken in bright sunlight, and with less sophisticated equipment than today's. Other pictures were too small or of very poor quality, and had to be left out.

I named other books, articles, and web resources that I consulted in the list of selected sources.

Chapter 2. June 6, 1944

1. Isaiah 40:31 (King James Version).

2. Luella Austin Parsons to Olive Titus, MS, TS, in the author's possession. September 11, 1943.

Chapter 3. Dinnertime

3. E. Dudley Parsons, Parsonalities, *Hennepin County (Hopkins, MN) Review,* April 1, 1943.

4. Parsons, Parsonalities, *Review,* March 25, 1943.

5. Ibid.

Chapter 4. Things Get Rearranged

6. Parsons, Parsonalities, *Review,* August 3, 1944.

Chapter 5. The Saturday Lunch Club

7. "Soviet Speaker Challenged by Woman," newspaper clipping in Saturday Lunch Club Collection, Minnesota History and James K. Hosmer Special Collections Library, Minneapolis Public Library, n.p., n.d., n.pag.

8. Earl Almquist, "Kline, Humphrey Join in Debate," *Minneapolis Tribune,* clipping in Saturday Lunch Club Collection, n.p., n.d., n.pag.

9. E. Dudley Parsons Sr. to E. Dudley Parsons Jr., *Parsons Family Letters*, August 8, 1931.

10. Parsons, Parsonalities, *Review*, July 16, 1942.

11. John A. Blatnik, M.C. [Member of Congress], to E. Dudley Parsons, Saturday Lunch Club Collection, June 21,1948.

Chapter 6. Grandpa's Rules for Reading

12. Walter Scott and David Laing, *Ivanhoe: A Romance* (New York: Modern Library, 2001) 1.

13. E. Dudley Parsons, *Heroes of the Northwest* [Minneapolis: Colwell Press, 1931, 1936], 56-57.

Chapter 10. Travel-itus

14. Parsons Sr. to Dudley and Luella Parsons, *Family Letters*, n.d. (ca. January, 1935.)

15. Ibid., September 30, 1934.

16. Ibid., October 5, 1934.

17. Ernest Parsons to Dudley and Luella Parsons, *Family Letters*, March 11, 1935.

18. Parsons Jr. to Parsons Sr. and Clara Dickey Parsons, *Family Letters*, November 14, 1935.

19. Parsons, Parsonalities, *Review*, October 10, 1940.

20. E. Dudley Parsons, *Encyclopedia Britannica Atlas Flyleaf Notes,* December 15, 1946, MS, electronic file, in the author's possession.

Chapter 11. Ernest's Shadow

21. Parsons, Parsonalities, *Review,* May 12, 1938.

22. Parsons, The Morningsider, *Review,* August 5, 1937.

23. Parsons, Parsonalities, *Review,* September 23, 1937.

24. E. Dudley Parsons, *Clara Dickey Parsons,* in the author's possession, n.p, n.d, n.pag.

25. E. Dudley Parsons Jr. *E. Dudley Parsons I Scrapbook,* in the author's possession, newspaper clipping, n.p., n.d., n.pag.

26. Newspaper clipping in photo album, in the author's possession, n.d., n.pag.

27. Parsons Sr. to Parsons Jr., *Family Letters,* May 22, 1932.

28. Ibid., October, 1932

29. Ibid., December 5, 1932

Chapter 12. The Garden

30. Parsons, The Morningsider, scrapbook clipping #67, in electronic file of 1935–1936 scrapbook, in the author's possession, n.d. Original is missing.

31. Parsons, Parsonalities, *Review,* March 8, 1945.

32. Ibid., May 23, 1940.

33. Ibid., June 18, 1942.

Chapter 13. A Climate Change

34. Luella Austin Parsons to Olive Titus, MS, TS, in the author's possession, September 11, 1943.

Chapter 18. Camel Cigarettes, Apricot Chair, Shakespeare

35. Parsons, *Flyleaf Notes,* December 3, 1950.

Chapter 20. Grandpa's Flight

36. Parsons, *Flyleaf Notes,* February 8, 1946.

37. Both postcards are in the author's possession.

38. "Ireland Is Prosperous, Parsons Finds," *Review,* September 27, 1951.

39. Parsons, Parsonalities, *Review,* November 8, 1951.

Chapter 21. Compelled to Write

40. Parsons Sr. to Parsons Jr., *Family Letters,* September 7, 1932. The original manuscript titled *Three Parsons* was later expanded to *Four Parsons.*

41. Ibid., June 20, 1930.

42. Clara Dickey Parsons to Dudley and Luella Parsons, *Family Letters*, November 20, 1934.

43. Parsons, Parsonalities, *Review*, October 21, 1937.

44. Parsons, The Morningsider, scrapbook clipping #73, electronic file, in the author's possession, n.d.

Chapter 22. *Bulgaria Today*

45. "Can't Win," *Minneapolis Sunday Tribune*, February 17, 1952.

46. 1953 Minnesota Statutes, Primary Elections, Section 202.43, p. 1787, Section 202.45, p. 1788, Minnesota Legislative Reference Library, TS. "The statutes are published in odd-numbered years but they would have been in effect for 1952 also." Email from David Schmidtke to author, February 28, 2011.

47. Secretary of State, Election Division, "An Inventory of Its Nominating Petitions," Section 112.B.20.12F Box 19. Minnesota Historical Society, Minnesota State Archives, TS. Email transmission from CI-St.Paul-SPPLInfo@ci.stpaul.mn.us.

48. Parsons, *Flyleaf Notes*, July 9, 1951.

49. E. Dudley Parsons, letter to the editor, *Daily Times*, April 11, 1948, clipping in Minnesota History and James K. Hosmer Special Collections Library, Minneapolis Public Library, n.p., n.pag.

50. Parsons, letter to the editor, *Minneapolis Tribune*, clipping in Minnesota History and James K. Hosmer Special Collections Library, Minneapolis Public Library, n.p., n.d., n.pag. (ca.

September 1938. The date is approximated, because the letter replies to another letter dated in September.)

51. Clipping in *E. Dudley Parsons I Scrapbook*, n.p., n.d., n.pag., in the author's possession.

52. Parsons, *Flyleaf Notes,* July 12, 1950.

Chapter 23. Grandpa's Last Journey

53. Walter Rauschenbusch, *Dare We Be Christians,* Pilgrim Press, 1914 (Eugene, Oregon: Wipf and Stock Publishers, 2000), 14.

54. "Funeral Rites Held Friday for E. Dudley Parsons," *Review,* September 25, 1952, clipping in *Parsons I Scrapbook*.

Chapter 24. *The Committee on the Russian Achievement*

55. Parsons, Parsonalities, *Review,* March 4, 1943.

56. "Duranty Articles Praised," clipping in Minnesota History and James K. Hosmer Special Collections Library, Minneapolis Public Library, n.p., n.d., n.pag.

57. Parsons Sr. to Parsons Jr., *Family Letters,* March 5, 1932.

Chapter 25. Scraps

58. L.S. Van Hook to W.F. Webster, in *Parsons I Scrapbook*, November 11, 1919, in author's possession.

59. Assistant Superintendent to E. Dudley Parsons, Ibid., June 19, 1923. The TS has no signature.

60. John M. Greer to W.F. Webster, Ibid., April 3, 1925.

61. Ruth S. Hill to "To Whom It May Concern," Ibid., April 24, 1940.

62. Clara Dickey Parsons to Parsons, Jr., *Family Letters,* August 1932.

Chapter 26. Church

63. Acts 4:32,34 (New Revised Standard Version).

Chapter 28. My Socialist Experiment

64. Acts 4:32,34–35 (New Revised Standard Version).

Chapter 36. A Family Founding Story

65. Henry William Parsons to Sarah Bennett Parsons, October 28, 1876, MS, Library of Congress, electronic file transcribed by James Dickey Parsons, in the author's possession.

66. Ibid., November 14, 1876.

Selected Sources

——

The following list is comprised of those books, articles, newspaper columns, family papers, and online materials that I read for background and consulted for this book. Sources I consulted for several stories, or for general understanding, are listed under the first title.

Chapter 1. Mystery Clues

Beevor, Antony. *Stalingrad*. New York: Viking, 1998.

Figes, Orlando. *Natasha's Dance: A Cultural History of Russia*. New York: Metropolitan Books, 2002.

———. *A People's Tragedy: The Russian Revolution, 1891–1924*. London: Jonathan Cape, 1996.

———. *The Whisperers: Private Life in Stalin's Russia*. New York: Metropolitan Books, 2002.

Hesterman, Paul C. *The History of Edina, Minnesota: From Settlement to Suburb*. Edina, MN: Burgess Publishing Company, 1988.

Massie, Robert K. *Catherine the Great: Portrait of a Woman*. New York: Random House, 2011.

Massie, Suzanne. *Land of the Firebird: The Beauty of Old Russia*. New York: Simon and Schuster, 1980.

Menand, Louis. "Getting Real: George F. Kennan's Cold War." The New Yorker, November14, 2011, 76. General Reference Center GOLD. http://go.galegroup.com/ps/i.do?id=GALE%7 CA272428215&v=2.1&u=fairfax_main&it=r&p+GRGM&sw=w Accessed February 3, 2014.

O'Clery, Conor. *Moscow December 25 1991: The Last Days of the Soviet Union.* New York: PublicAffairs, 2011.

Parsons, E. Dudley. *Encyclopedia Britannica Atlas Flyleaf Notes.* MS, 1935–1946. In the author's possession.

———. The Morningsider. *Hennepin County [Hopkins, MN] Review.* September 24, 1936 through February 1, 1940.

———. Parsonalities. *Hennepin County [Hopkins, MN] Review.* February 8, 1940 through October 11, 1951.

———. The State of the World. *Hennepin County [Hopkins, MN] Review.* July 11, 1946; September 26, 1946; October 3, 1946; October 17, 1946; October 24, 1946; February 6, 1947; and May 5, 1947.

Parsons Family Letters (to and from Erick Austin, Hildegard Austin Hoffman, Clara Dickey Parsons, Edgar Parsons, Ernest Parsons, E. Dudley Parsons Sr., E. Dudley Parsons Jr. 1930–1937). Transcribed by James Dickey Parsons. N.d. MS, TS, and electronic file. In the author's possession.

Price, Barbara. *Hopscotch: A Morningside Childhood.* Santa Clara, CA: DeHART'S Printing Services Corporation, 2002.

Remnick, David. *Lenin's Tomb: The Last Days of the Soviet Empire.* New York: Random House, 1993.

———. *Resurrection: The Struggle for a New Russia.* New York: Random House, 1997.

Volkov, Solomon M., and Antonina W. Bouis. *Shostakovich and Stalin.* New York: A.A. Knopf, 2004.

von Bremzen, Anya. *Mastering the Art of Soviet Cooking: A Memoir of Food and Longing.* New York: Crown Publishers, 2013.

Chapter 3. Dinnertime

Culver, John C., and John Hyde. *American Dreamer: The Life and Times of Henry A. Wallace.* New York: Norton, 2000.

Lazarro, Joseph. "Bengal Famine of 1943 – A Man-Made Holocaust." *International Business Times.* February 22, 2013. http://www.ibtimes.com/bengal-famine-1943-man-made-holocaust-1100525. Accessed May 4, 2015.

Chapter 4. Things Get Rearranged

Douglas, Marjorie Myers. *The Gathering Together: Glimpses Into* [sic] *the History of Edina Morningside Community Church (UCC) 1902–2002.* Edina, MN: Book Mobile, 2002.

Parsons, E. Dudley. To War Production Board, Washington, D.C. Letter of Application December 4, 1944. TS in *E. Dudley Parsons I Scrapbook.* In the author's possession.

War Production Board to E. Dudley Parsons. Letter. February 7, 1945. TS in *E. Dudley Parsons I Scrapbook.* In the author's possession.

Chapter 5. The Saturday Lunch Club

Almquist, Earl. "Kline, Humphrey Join in Debate," *Minneapolis Tribune.* Clipping in Saturday Lunch Club Collection, Minnesota History and James K. Hosmer Special Collections Library, Minneapolis Public Library. N.p. N.d.

Blatnik, M.C. [Member of Congress], John A., to E. Dudley Parsons Sr. Letter. June 21, 1948. Saturday Lunch Club Collection, Minnesota History and James K. Hosmer Special Collections Library, Minneapolis Public Library.

Everts, William P. "Defying Enumeration: Sylvanus A. Stockwell of Minneapolis," *Hennepin History* (Fall, 1995): 5 – 23.

Lemann, Nicholas. "Spy Wars: The Real Legacy of Soviet Spying in America." *The New Yorker,* July 27, 2009.

Leonard, Wm. E. *The Saturday Lunch Club of Minneapolis: A Brief History.* Minneapolis, MN: 1927. Pamphlet in Saturday Lunch Club Collection, Minnesota History and James K. Hosmer Special Collections Library, Minneapolis Public Library.

LeSueur, Marian, and E. Dudley Parsons. *The Liberal Movement in the North Middle-West and The Integration of the Saturday Lunch Club with That Movement.* Minneapolis, MN: N.p., 1951. In the author's possession.

LeSueur, Meridel. *Crusaders: The Radical Legacy of Marian and Arthur LeSueur.* St. Paul: Minnesota Historical Society Press, 1984. Reprint. Originally published New York: Blue Heron Press, 1955.

Smith, Douglas. *Former People: The Final Days of the Russian Aristocracy.* New York: Farrar Strauss and Giroux, 2012.

"The Saturday Lunch Club Program Notes 1930–1952." Transcription by James Dickey Parsons. October, 2001. TS and electronic file. In the author's possession. Selected reminder postcards in Saturday Lunch Club Collection, Minnesota History and James K. Hosmer Special Collections Library, Minneapolis Public Library.

Wingate, Earl. "Saturday Luncheon Club Notes 40th Anniversary." *Minneapolis Tribune.* February 13, 1949. Clipping in Saturday Lunch Club Collection, Minnesota History and James K. Hosmer Special Collections Library, Minneapolis Public Library.

Chapter 6. Grandpa's Rules for Reading

Curran, Hugh A., and E. Dudley Parsons. *The Government of Minnesota.* Minneapolis, MN: 1934.

Parsons, E. Dudley. *Heroes of the Northwest.* [Minneapolis, Minnesota: The Colwell Press], 1931, 1936

———. *Making Minneapolis.* [Minneapolis, Minnesota]: 1926.

———. *Seeing Minneapolis.* [Minneapolis, Minnesota]: 1948.

————. *The Story of Minneapolis.* [Minneapolis, Minnesota: The Colwell Press], 1913.

Scott, Walter and David Laing. *Ivanhoe: A Romance.* New York: Modern Library, 2001.

Chapter 7. Excursions with Grandpa

The Cleveland Museum of Art. *Masterpieces from the Berlin Museums Exhibited in Cooperation with the Department of the Army of the United States of America.* Cleveland: The Artcraft Printing Company, 1948.

Wikipedia. s.v. "Mendota Bridge." http://en.wikipedia.org/wiki/Mendota_Bridge. Accessed October 20, 2012.

Chapter 11. Ernest's Shadow

Parsons, E. Dudley. *Clara Dickey Parsons.* N.p., n.d., n.pag. In the author's possession.

Parsons, E. Dudley, Jr. *E. Dudley Parsons I Scrapbook.* In the author's possession.

Chapter 13. A Climate Change

Parsons, Luella Austin to Olive Titus. Letter. TS from MS. September 11, 1943. In the author's possession.

Chapter 16. Turbulence

Time Magazine. "Education: Minneapolis on Strike." March 8, 1948.

Chapter 23. *Bulgaria Today*

1953 Minnesota Statutes. Primary Elections. Section 202.43, p. 1787; Section 202.45, p. 1788. Minnesota Legislative Reference Library.

An Inventory of Its Nominating Petitions. Secretary of State, Election Division, Minnesota State Archives. Section 112.B.20.13B Box 19.

Mitau, G. Theodore. "The Democratic Farmer–Labor Party Schism of 1948." *Minnesota History*, 34, no. 5 (1955), 187–194.

———. *Politics in Minnesota.* Minneapolis, MN: University of Minnesota Press: 1960, 1970.

Chapter 23. Grandpa's Last Journey

Rauschenbusch, Walter. *Dare We Be Christians.* Pilgrim Press, 1914. Eugene, Oregon: Wipf and Stock Publishers, 2000.

Chapter 24. The Committee on the Russian Achievement

Conquest, Robert. *The Great Terror: A Reassessment.* New York, Oxford: Oxford University Press, 1990.

Davies, Joseph E. *Mission to Moscow.* New York: Pocket Books Inc., 1941.

Hughes, Langston. *I Wonder As I Wander: An Autobiographical Journey.* New York: Hill and Wang, 1993.

Parsons, E. Dudley, Chairman. *Report of the Committee on the Russian Achievement: As Presented to the Saturday Lunch Club on May Seventh, Nineteen-Thirty-six [sic].* Minneapolis, Minnesota: Saturday Lunch Club, 1936. First Edition. In the author's possession.

Thomas, D. M. *Alexander Solzhenitsyn: A Century in His Life.* New York: St. Martin's Press, 1998.

Chapter 27. Interrogation

American Peace Crusade, Minneapolis Chapter, to National Delegates Assembly for Peace, Washington, D.C. Letter. March 26, 1952. TS. In the author's possession.

Chapter 28. My Socialist Experiment

Wikipedia. s.v. "Greensboro sit-ins." http://www.en.wkipedia.org/wiki/Greensboro_sit-ins. Accessed November 26, 2010, and May 4, 2015.

Chapter 32. Bright Glade

Wilson, A.N. *Tolstoy.* New York: Norton, 1988.

Chapter 34. Hide and Seek

Yates, Gayle Graham. "LeSueur, Meridel." In *Notable American Women, Vol. 5,* edited by Susan Ware. Cambridge, Mass: Belknap Press, 2004.

Chapter 36. A Family Founding Story

Parsons, E. Dudley. *Four Parsons: A View of Certain Aspects of Life in the United States Since 1876.* TS. In the author's possession.
Parsons, Henry William. *Diaries and Letters.* 1873–1887. MS. Library of Congress. Electronic file transcribed by James Dickey Parsons. In the author's possession.

Made in the USA
San Bernardino, CA
14 January 2016